D0416792

# 101 Cocktails

## to Try Before You Die

# 101 Cocktails

## to Try Before You Die

François Monti

An Hachette UK Company
www.hachette.co.uk

First published in Great Britain in
2016 by Cassell, a division of
Octopus Publishing Group Ltd
Carmelite House
50 Victoria Embankment
London EC4Y 0DZ
www.octopusbooks.co.uk
www.octopusbooksusa.com

Previously published in French by Dunod
in 2015

Copyright © Dunod, Paris, 2015
Design and layout copyright © Octopus
Publishing Group Limited 2016

Distributed in the US by
Hachette Book Group
1290 Avenue of the Americas
4th and 5th Floors
New York, NY 10104

Distributed in Canada by
Canadian Manda Group
664 Annette St.
Toronto, Ontario, Canada M6S 2C8

All rights reserved. No part of this work
may be reproduced or utilized in any form
or by any means, electronic or mechanical,
including photocopying, recording or by
any information storage and retrieval
system, without the prior written
permission of the publisher.

ISBN 978 1 84403 877 0

A CIP catalogue record for this book is
available from the British Library.

Printed and bound in China

10 9 8 7 6 5 4 3 2

Group Publishing Director Denise Bates
Editor Pauline Bache
Designers Jeremy Tilston and Jaz Bahra
Production Controller Allison Gonsalves
Translation by JMS Books LLP

Standard level spoon measurements are
used in all recipes.
1 tablespoon = one 15ml spoon
1 teaspoon = one 5ml spoon

The Department of Health advises that
eggs should not be consumed raw. This book
contains some recipes made with raw eggs.
It is prudent for vulnerable people such as
pregnant and nursing mothers, invalids and
the elderly to avoid these recipes.

This book includes recipes made with nuts
and nut derivatives. It is advisable for those
with known allergic reactions to nuts and
nut derivatives to avoid these recipes.

It is also prudent to check the labels of
pre-prepared ingredients for the possible
inclusion of nut derivatives.

The UK Health Department recommends
that you do not regularly exceed 2–3 units
of alcohol in a day, a unit being defined as
10ml of pure alcohol, the equivalent of a
single measure (25ml/¾fl oz) of spirits.
Those who regularly drink more than
this run an increasingly significant risk
of illness and death from a number of
conditions. In addition, women who are
pregnant or trying to conceive should avoid
drinking alcohol.

The U.S. Department of Health and
Human Services recommends that men
do not regularly exceed 2 drinks a day and
women 1 drink a day, a drink being defined
as 0.5 oz of pure alcohol, the equivalent of
1.5 oz of 80-proof distilled spirits. Those
who regularly drink more than this run
an increasingly significant risk of illness
and death from a number of conditions.
In addition, women who are pregnant or
trying to conceive should avoid drinking
alcohol.

# Contents

# Introduction

From time immemorial, we have mixed drinks. The earliest wines were flavoured with herbs and later with spices, as were the first beers. The advent of spirits saw the gradual development of drinks served with fruits, water or spices. Historically, punches were the first family of this type of drink to become popular, at the beginning of the 18th century. The Sling and the Julep followed and then, towards the end of the 18th century, the cocktail arrived, although at the time this was, according to its earliest definition published in 1806, just one kind of mixed drink (spirits, sugar, water and aromatic bitters, to be exact). It was only later, between 1860 and 1920, that the meaning of the word 'cocktail' would change, eventually encompassing all alcoholic mixes.

To some extent this book is a history of this evolution. With one or two exceptions, it features only recipes developed after 1806. With the 101 factsheets I will try to guide you through the history of the cocktail (in the current sense of the word), from its medicinal beginnings to the real renaissance we see today. I will recount some of the early glories of the art of the bar, when styles and families of drinks were still strictly separated, and discuss the classic era of the American cocktail that between 1870 and 1920 gave rise to some of the most iconic recipes in its history (Martini, Manhattan, etc.).

And, of course, we will also look at what was happening outside the United States, particularly in Cuba, where the local *cantineros* (bartenders) created a ground-breaking style (Daiquiri, Mary Pickford and other cocktails), and also in Europe, especially in the Golden Age, which for us means the years 1920 to 1930, when Americans were under the yoke of Prohibition. The end of that dry period led to the birth of the Tiki style, a strange assortment of Americanized Caribbean cocktails, dispensed in bars decorated in a South Pacific-inspired style, and I include several typical recipes.

The period from 1960 to 1980 saw a decline in the art of mixing, but I don't overlook several cocktails that emerged during this time which – unfortunately or otherwise – everyone knows. Finally, a number of recipes (approximately twenty) help us to understand how the cocktail renaissance came about nearly twenty years ago in New York and London.

The 101 recipes collected here are not meant to offer an accurate picture of the spirits used in today's bars. Indeed, some will say that there is too much of this sort and not enough of that. My choice has been guided by three considerations: the recipes should be relatively easy to make at home; viewed together, they should give a better understanding of what the word cocktail means; finally and most importantly, they should give me with the chance to tell you some stories. Obviously, drinking is a social act. It's also a cultural one. It is not, in my view, desirable to deal with it from an exclusively technical standpoint (explaining how to make the cocktails, enumerating the ingredients, and so on). The cocktail is the history of the women and men who created them, the places where they were born, the products on which they are based and the people who drink them. And the world of the bar has generated lots of impressive stories, although, regrettably, some are myths and legends. Without taking away the magic (or claiming to be infallible), my hope is to provide reliable accounts that will enhance the understanding of the origins of drinks, and thereby enjoyment of their consumption.

I am no bartender. Initially, I was just someone, like you, who likes to drink cocktails. Then I decided to take it further and over the past few years I have contributed many articles to magazines, websites and brands. The recipes are not mine. I have collected them over the years from various sources. They suit my preferences but do adapt them slightly if they are not wholly to your taste. The recipes should be respected but they are not sacrosanct: as in cookery, everybody changes something. The brands that some of the recipes call for are generally included as suggestions. They are always excellent products that work well in the recipe in question, but feel free to use what you have available. The tasting notes are also guidelines, especially since they vary depending on the ingredients. Nor should the human factor be overlooked, it is an important element of the final product (precision, temperature, dilution ...) that may considerably alter the perception of the cocktail. As for the methods of mixing cocktails, I have tried hard to suggest the shortest possible recipes. So as not to get lost, I advise any reader who is starting out to turn first to Cocktail Techniques on page 212. It offers a brief introduction to the craft of the cocktail.

Finally, this book is organized alphabetically but the recipes could equally have been arranged chronologically. Read them in the order that suits you best, try the cocktails that appeal to you most and discover more than two centuries of mixed drinks. I hope that the journey will be a revelation, giving you a better understanding of the drinks, providing insights in the years to come into those on the menu of your favourite bars – where they come from and how they have evolved. Ultimately, these 101 cocktails are a tribute to the ingenuity of an important profession, albeit one that has been too often looked down upon, and the drinks they offered to all those who visited their bars over the years for a brief respite from the cares of the world.

# 1

# 20th-Century Cocktail

INGREDIENTS

45ml (1½fl oz) Aviation
Gin, 20ml (¾fl oz) Lillet,
20ml (¾fl oz) fresh
lemon juice, 15ml
(½fl oz) Crème de cacao,
lemon peel or white
chocolate to serve
(optional)

The fact that the 20th-Century Cocktail did not make an appearance until 1937 is just one of the oddities of the world of cocktails. Yet another is that it was apparently created by a British bartender called C.A. Tuck, although it was named in honour of a train that ran between New York and Chicago from 1902. Perhaps all is explained by the 1934 release of Howard Hawks's film *Twentieth Century*, in which John Barrymore, playing a Broadway producer on the skids, attempts to escape his creditors by train and to resurrect his failing career by re-signing his star, the great Carole Lombard.

The impact of Hollywood on world imagination was already a reality, and the number of cocktails inspired by its stars or its movies was substantial. The 20th-Century cocktail comes from the *Café Royal Cocktail Book* by William J. Tarling, the first manual of the United Kingdom Bartenders' Guild, founded in 1933. It's a cocktail of its time: it contains Lillet, or rather Kina (for quinine) Lillet as it was then called, probably a lot more bitter than the version we know today. The Kina Lillet that prevailed among the kings of mixology of the time no longer exists. For a more 'authentic' result it can be replaced by other aperitif wines containing quinine, such as Kina L'Aéro d'Or. Or just use the current Lillet: the cocktail will have less depth but will be no less excellent and won't cost you an arm and a leg.

If you settle for this last option, once the cocktails are prepared keep the bottle of Lillet chilled (this goes for all fortified wines such as vermouth, Dubonnet, sherry) and drink it as an aperitif, over ice with a slice of orange. You won't regret it.

PREPARATION

**Shake in a cocktail shaker**

TYPE OF GLASS

**Serve in a cocktail glass**

PRESENTATION

**Garnish with a twist of lemon peel or serve with white chocolate**

DIFFICULTY

**Moderate**

STYLE

**Rich, luscious cocktail**

TASTE

**Round, with cocoa and orange flavours**

**FINISH**

**Medium length, cocoa to the fore, slight acidity**

# 2

# Air Mail

INGREDIENTS
.................................

30ml (1fl oz) Havana
Club 3 Años, 15ml
(½fl oz) honey, 15ml
(½fl oz) lime juice,
Champagne, lemon or
orange peel to serve

Cocktails are generally associated with sophistication but this was not always the case. It is thought that the oldest Cuban cocktail is the Cancháchara. It was created during the Ten Years' War of 1868–78, fought against Spain by Cubans seeking independence. The cocktail is a mixture of local, easily found ingredients: aguardiente made from sugar cane, honey (or molasses or cane juice), lime and water. Drunk on cold mornings in the sierra, it gave the rebels, the Mambises, energy and courage when defeat appeared inevitable and nourishment unavailable.

But the origins of this drink undoubtedly go back even further: all its ingredients are to be found on sugar-cane plantations and it's easy to imagine African slaves mixing it so that time might pass more quickly and they could forget their condition for a while. To understand the scope of the country's evolution, you need to project yourself forward more than fifty years: no slaves, sky-high sugar-cane prices, a developing middle class and increasingly numerous urbanization projects.

Traces of this period can still be seen in the Vedado and Marianao quarters of Havana. The Champagne that arrived in New York before Prohibition reached Cuba at the same time as commercial aviation; Champagne bubbles replaced the water in the Cancháchara and the Air Mail was born. Bacardi, tireless promoter of American tourism even during the years following the 1934 sugar-cane crash, included it in its brochures. It can still be found in some bars nowadays – you'll understand why when you try it. Be careful, however, three Air Mails and it's you who will be flying, with no guarantee that you will reach your destination....

**PREPARATION**

**Shake in a cocktail shaker (except for the Champagne)**

**TYPE OF GLASS**

**Serve in a Champagne flute and top up with Champagne**

**PRESENTATION**

**Garnish with a twist of lemon or orange peel**

**DIFFICULTY**

**Moderate**

**STYLE**

**Champagne Cuban-style**

**TASTE**

**Mellow yet acidulated**

**FINISH**

The honey and Champagne dominate, with light molasses notes

# 3

# Amaretto Sour

40ml (1¼fl oz) amaretto,
20ml (¾fl oz) cask-
strength bourbon,
30ml (1fl oz) lemon juice,
1 teaspoon sugar syrup,
egg white, lemon or
maraschino cherries
to serve (optional)

Ok, we admit it: we're into dry cocktails. So to drink a cocktail that's clearly been created by a brand for promotional purposes, one with amaretto as the main ingredient, a very (very) sweet almond-tasting liqueur to which – according to the original recipe – sugar syrup still has to be added, doesn't exactly bode well. Diabetes alert! However, against all odds this is a rather popular cocktail and we're ready to bet that plenty of cupboards contain more bottles of good amaretto than of good gin. What is to be done?

Well, for a start, forget the syrup: the liqueur is enough to lower the acidity and balance the cocktail. Next, why not add two or three dashes of Angostura, to give it more depth? Fine, but not enough, one wants to say. At this point the American bartender Jeffrey Morgenthaler steps in. He's known above all for his ability to simplify the most complicated techniques. Confronted with the problem of the Amaretto Sour, he quickly saw that it lacked alcoholic strength and character. His solution? Drag the Amaretto Sour onto Whiskey Sour territory, with a little more amaretto and some bourbon. For the latter, he recommends something very strong: a 60 per cent ABV, cask-strength (also known as barrel-proof), with no water to dilute the alcohol level before bottling. It's hard to find and it's rather expensive, thanks to taxes. But the result, while still sugary, is worth the trouble; it is considerably more powerful and flavourful.

For a more traditional version, use the following proportions: 50ml (1¾fl oz) amaretto, 30ml (1fl oz) lemon juice, 1 dash of Angostura, egg white. But why bother? There's no comparison; the great Jeffrey was not wrong when he claimed to make the best Amaretto Sour in the world.

PREPARATION

**Shake in a cocktail shaker**

TYPE OF GLASS

**Serve in an Old Fashioned glass filled with ice cubes**

PRESENTATION

**Garnish with a twist of lemon peel or maraschino cherries (optional)**

DIFFICULTY

**Difficult**

STYLE

**Variation on Whiskey Sour**

TASTE

**Rich vanilla and almond flavours**

**FINISH**

**Average length, with almond and lemon notes**

# Americano

INGREDIENTS
......................

30ml (1fl oz) Campari,
30ml (1fl oz) red
vermouth, soda water,
orange slices to serve

Italians are kings of the aperitif. It's impossible to stroll through a North Italian town in the late afternoon without being tempted by a table laden with focaccia, bruschetta, charcuterie, olives .... Of course, to sample them means ordering a drink, but which one? While the Spritz, more or less well prepared, has become the fashionable drink on all terraces of the western world and although cocktail lovers tend to prefer the stronger and more grown-up pleasures of the Negroni (of which more later), most of the time I would plump for a true classic, too often ignored on this side of the Alps: the Americano. It's a recipe that harks back to an era when the American cocktail had not yet taken over in Europe. Of course, mixes existed but they came in simpler forms.

The Americano was born in the middle of the 19th century, when it was known as the Milano–Torino, after the sources of its two base products: vermouth (Turin) and bitters (Milan). However, Campari was not the original choice for the bitters. In fact, it is said that the much more bitter Fernet Branca had that honour. Indeed, this recipe works well with any Italian bitter, especially those whose profile comes from orange bitters. The name of the drink is reputed to have changed in the early twentieth century. Some say this was because American tourists liked it so much, others that it refers to its bitterness (from the Italian *amarricante* – that which embitters).

I have a few theories as to the value of these explanations – chiefly, I wonder what etymological evolution could turn an adjective into a noun to which it bore no resemblance, and in a very few years to boot. But, frankly, who asks such a question at 5pm in the shadow of Milan's Duomo or on the Place San Carlo in Turin? Not me and certainly not you. How do you say 'Waiter!' in Italian?

**PREPARATION**

**Mix in a Collins glass**

**PRESENTATION**

**Serve over ice, garnish with slices of orange**

**DIFFICULTY**

**Easy**

**STYLE**

**Refreshing aperitif, slightly bitter**

**TASTE**

**Bitter oranges, herbs and spices but relatively smooth**

FINISH

Light, but fresh over the bitterness

# Army & Navy

INGREDIENTS
.......................................

50ml (1¾fl oz) gin,
20ml (¾fl oz) orgeat
(almond syrup), 20ml
(¾fl oz) lemon juice,
2 dashes Angostura
bitters (optional),
lemon to serve

Creative bartenders always amaze first-time clients, often with good reason. What the client doesn't necessarily know is that, as in fiction – which some say has just seven basic plot lines – the number of basic drinks templates is also limited; rare is the cocktail that doesn't bear some fleeting resemblance to another. One of the cocktail families with the most twists or variations is the Sours. The basic formula is simple: spirits, sugar, citrus fruit. The syrup can be changed, the fruit can be varied or the degree of acidity altered, as can the spirits, of course. That's how the Margarita and the Sidecar (*see* page 186) were born.

We'll return to these later, but for the present let us concentrate on the simplest variation. It appeared for the first time in 1948 in a book by David Embury, a passionate cocktail enthusiast. Take a Gin Sour (gin, sugar syrup and fresh lemon) as it was drunk during the 1860s in the US (or, rather, in 1900 – in 1860 the gin would have been a Dutch genever or have had extra sugar). Replace the simple (yet effective) sugar syrup with orgeat, an almond syrup flavoured with orange flower water that owes its name to the barley (*orge* in French) decoction originally used to make it. This will give you a Gin Sour with orgeat, in other words an Army & Navy, which may owe its name to an American football match played by teams from the army and naval academies.

The transformation is extraordinary, yet it's a recipe so simple that any cocktail lover should be able to play with it. I like to add two dashes of Angostura bitters for more depth. But try it without. Adjust the proportions of lemon juice and syrup to your taste. Discover not THE formula but YOUR formula. This is how you can begin to personalize your cocktails.

PREPARATION

**Shake in a cocktail shaker**

TYPE OF GLASS

**Serve in a cocktail glass**

PRESENTATION

**Garnish with a twist of lemon peel**

DIFFICULTY

**Moderate**

STYLE

**An easy aperitif**

TASTE

**Gin and almond**

**FINISH**

Refreshing, with almond and lemon notes

# 6 Aviation

**INGREDIENTS**

60ml (2fl oz) Aviation gin, 20ml (¾fl oz) lemon juice, 15ml (½fl oz) maraschino liqueur, 1 teaspoon Crème de violette, 1 black cherry

After more than thirty years in the wilderness, the art of the cocktail saw a revival in the US during the 1990s. In truth, most of the damage had been done much earlier, during Prohibition. Contrary to the popular image, that era was grim and charmless, and certainly not a golden age where cocktails were prepared in sexy speakeasies (clandestine bars). On the contrary, it was a catastrophe for the cocktail: the older bartenders retired, the rest went into exile or changed professions, no successors were trained, many drinks brands folded and products disappeared for decades. The tradition of good drinking and good products was lost.

When a new generation decided, at the turn of the century, to raise the quality of cocktails, they turned to pre-Prohibition books, notably one written in 1917 by Hugh Ensslin. Very little is known about Ensslin but his work represents a kind of 'state of the nation' for the American cocktail, before the axe fell on the whole industry. One of his recipes became an icon of the cocktail renaissance: the Aviation.

The Aviation was still vaguely known but little made at the turn of the century because it didn't seem very inspiring: gin, lemon juice and maraschino (Marasca cherry liqueur). But the first Indiana Joneses of the cocktail deduced from Ensslin's little-known book that a vital ingredient was missing from their recipes: Crème de violette, impossible to find in the US since Prohibition. Dedicated bartenders who managed to lay their hands on this product discovered a splendid sky-blue-coloured cocktail. The name finally made sense. A forgotten historic recipe, a lost ingredient: that's the formula on which this cocktail's revival was based. Take care, however, the Aviation is a cocktail where it's difficult to get the balance right and it demands top-quality liqueurs.

PREPARATION

Shake in a cocktail shaker

TYPE OF GLASS

Serve in a cocktail glass

PRESENTATION

Garnish with a black cherry

DIFFICULTY

Difficult

STYLE

Floral aperitif

TASTE

Lightly acidic with violet notes

FINISH

The maraschino's herbaceous notes predominate

21

# 7

# Bamboo

INGREDIENTS
........................................

45ml (1½fl oz) Fino or
Oloroso sherry, 45ml
(1½fl oz) dry vermouth,
2 dashes Angostura
bitters, 1 dash orange
bitters, orange peel or
1 olive to serve

Logically the name of your cocktail should relate to its ingredients, where it was created or perhaps to a fashionable cultural phenomenon. How, therefore, does one explain the Bamboo, which mixes sherry, French vermouth and bitters and was created by an American bartender of German origin? Louis Eppinger popularized this recipe at the Grand Hotel in ... Yokohama, where he arrived in 1890. American bartender, Spanish and French ingredients, luxury Japanese hotel. Indeed, at the end of the 19th century the cocktail was already a global phenomenon.

Émile Lefeuvre's *Méthode pour composer soi-même les boissons américaines* ('How to make your own American drinks'), the first book of cocktail recipes published in France, appeared in 1889, the same year as the French Exposition Universelle, which had as its symbol the Eiffel Tower. In London Leo Engel, a compatriot of Eppinger, officiated behind the bar of the Criterion, an establishment which still exists, in the middle of Piccadilly Circus.

To return to the Bamboo: use red vermouth instead of dry and you get an Adonis, the Bamboo's big brother, in fact. The variations on these two formulas are innumerable but these are the two cocktails that have come down to posterity. Both are excellent, and their base consists of no ingredients above 20 per cent ABV. In fact, taking dilution into account, the Bamboo probably measures around 12 per cent ABV – less than some wines. It's a delicious aperitif that won't send the drinker to sleep, has all the elegance of a cocktail and remains absolutely simple to prepare. Expect to see more and more recipes of this kind: low-alcohol drinks that enhance the qualities of Europe's marvellous fortified wines.

PREPARATION

**Stir in a mixing glass**

TYPE OF GLASS

**Serve in a cocktail glass**

PRESENTATION

**Garnish with a twist of orange peel or an olive**

DIFFICULTY

**Moderate**

STYLE

**Light, dry aperitif**

TASTE

**Slightly herbaceous, with almond notes**

FINISH

**Medium, dry, nutty and slightly orange**

# 8

# Bamboo Crane

### INGREDIENTS

50ml (1¾fl oz) Nikka From The Barrel Japanese whisky, 15ml (½fl oz) Carpano Antica Formula vermouth, 1½ teaspoons Pedro Ximénez sherry, ½ teaspoon Bonal, 1 dash Peychaud's bitters, 3 drops Bob's Abbotts bitters, maraschino cherry or ½ dried fig to serve, orange peel to serve

Cooking, like cocktails, often makes one think of techniques: caramelizing, smoking, infusing, reducing .... The two worlds also share certain philosophies or – some would say – fashions. In restaurants, it's often more important to know who made your cheese rather than its appellation, or what the pig ate during the last months of its life; likewise, bartenders can also become extremely specific about the provenance of the ingredients they use.

So it's no longer just a question of gin, but gin produced in a certain way (and if the bartender is any good he will give you a sensible explanation for his choice). And in the quest for authenticity that is also found in cooking (and even though the concept is highly problematic), bartenders today are turning to products that used to be popular with the masses but are currently ignored by the public and the profession. Joseph Akhavan is one of those people who likes to work in the kitchen (his homemade preparations are well-known) and carefully selects the products he will use.

You won't find 120 whiskies in his bar but you can be sure that that the range has been carefully chosen. In his excellent Bamboo Crane you'll find a quality Japanese whisky that is within reach of the hip and cool. Tradition is represented by Carpano Antica Formula (a vanilla vermouth that has been made for 120 years and is now all the rage in bars worldwide), Pedro Ximénez sherry and Bonal, a divine gentian-flavoured aperitif that, sadly, is better known to collectors of vintage labels than to drinkers. Joseph also calls on Bob Petrie's craft bitters, a not entirely faithful but wholly excellent reproduction of a brand that disappeared with Prohibition. If you can't get them, use Angostura – the effect will be different but the cocktail will still be very good.

## PREPARATION

**Stir in a mixing glass**

## TYPE OF GLASS

**Serve in an Old Fashioned or a cocktail glass**

## PRESENTATION

**Garnish with a maraschino cherry or half a dried fig, and squeeze the oils from a twist of orange peel over the cocktail**

## DIFFICULTY

**Difficult**

## STYLE

**Full-bodied cocktail**

## TASTE

**Medicinal, herbaceous, with smoked notes**

**FINISH**

A touch of bitterness balanced by the Pedro Ximénez notes. Lingering herbiness

# Bee's Knees

INGREDIENTS

50ml (1¾fl oz) Aviation
gin, 20ml (¾fl oz) lemon
juice, 20ml (¾fl oz)
honey, lemon peel
to serve

Born in Austria at the end of the 19th century, Frank Meier made his reputation in pre-Prohibition America. As his job became illegal, in 1921 he wound up at the bar of the Paris Ritz, which made him famous, influential and rich. Frank was meticulous, obsessive and undoubtedly a bit of a miser. He preferred to work in the room, like a maître d'hôtel, rather than behind his bar. He could rely on a famous team, which may already have included Bertin, one of Hemingway's favourite bartenders, who claimed to have liberated the place in 1944.

During the war, the Ritz was one of the rare Parisian palaces open to the public. It is said that Meier, who was rumoured to be half-Jewish, acted as a postbox for some Wehrmacht conspirators implicated in the failed attempt to assassinate Hitler on 20 July 1944, a month before Paris was liberated. It was also said that Meier several times helped clients who were members of the Resistance, Allied soldiers or Jews. Stories abound although they are difficult to confirm since he died in 1947. What is certain is that behind the severe moustache and the white waistcoat lurked an unusual personality, whose influence went far beyond his establishment.

In 1936 he published a book entitled – with no trace of false modesty – *The Artistry of Mixing Drinks*. It was printed in a very limited edition that ended up in the collections of his most distinguished clients. It includes one of his creations, the Bee's Knees, whose name was a popular expression adopted by the flappers, those young, liberated, post-WW1 women. Experiment with different honeys, and you will discover a different cocktail every time. But a word of advice: dilute it well with the lemon juice before adding the ice cubes, otherwise it will solidify on contact with the cold ice.

PREPARATION

**Shake in a cocktail shaker**

TYPE OF GLASS

**Serve in a cocktail glass**

PRESENTATION

**Garnish with a twist of lemon peel**

DIFFICULTY

**Difficult**

STYLE

**Light, luscious cocktail**

TASTE

**Good honey taste, but with a touch of dryness from the juniper**

**FINISH**

**Long and silky, balanced between lemon and honey**

# Bensonhurst

### INGREDIENTS

60ml (2fl oz) rye
whiskey, 30ml (1fl oz) dry
vermouth, 2 teaspoons
maraschino liqueur,
1 teaspoon Cynar, lemon
peel to serve (optional)

Around 1880 a bartender invented the Manhattan. Twenty years later another bartender invented the Brooklyn (a Manhattan with dry vermouth and Picon). Then – nothing, apart from the Bronx (not very good but strangely popular for many years).

Fast forward to 2004. The cocktail renaissance is in full swing in New York. Young bartenders are fascinated by the pre-Prohibition classics, including the Manhattan and the Brooklyn. Vincenzo Errico creates a maraschino Manhattan (something that would have been perfectly normal 120 years earlier, since the recipe had not then been fixed in its 'classic' version, but let it pass). He called it the Red Hook, after another New York district.

The virus spread: Slope, Little Italy, Brooklyn Heights and Cobble Hill followed. It even leaped over to New Jersey with the Newark. Each time, twists to the two models. Good cocktails, on the whole, including two authentic modern classics: Michael McIlroy's Greenpoint (60ml/2fl oz rye whiskey, 15ml/½fl oz red vermouth, 15ml/½fl oz yellow Chartreuse, 2 dashes of Angostura and 1 of orange bitters: it's divine) and the Bensonhurst. This was created in 2006 by Chad Solomon at the Pegu Club. It's clearly a slightly modified Brooklyn. The two cocktails share the same core: namely rye, dry vermouth and maraschino. The difference is that while the Brooklyn's bitterness comes from the very French Picon, for the Bensonhurst Solomon turned to Italy and one of its famous *amari* (bitter liqueurs), namely Cynar.

It's just a small twist, but it changes the whole thing. However, don't kid yourself that your liver will stand up to it better just because the Cynar contains some artichoke.

**PREPARATION**

Stir in a mixing glass

**TYPE OF GLASS**

Serve in a cocktail glass

**PRESENTATION**

Express the oil from a twist of lemon peel over the surface (optional)

**DIFFICULTY**

Moderate

**STYLE**

Sweet, bitter and strong aperitif

**TASTE**

Intense, spicy, balsamic, slightly sugary

**FINISH**

Medium, subtly floral, herby and bitter

29

# 11

# Benton's Old Fashioned

INGREDIENTS

60ml (2fl oz) bacon-infused Four Roses Yellow bourbon (see right), 2 teaspoons maple syrup, 2 dashes Angostura bitters, orange peel to serve

Things now get a little bizarre. Having rediscovered the recipes of the past, bartenders turned to the future, and the future is cooking and science. One of the magicians of this new school is called Don Lee and his hour of glory arrived in 2008 when he decided to do a 'fat-wash', a technique that was first applied to the cocktail by Eben Freeman.

Inspired by the pastry chef of the restaurant where he worked, Freeman created a rum with *beurre noisette* (brown butter). This involved infusing the spirit with a fatty liquid. For his cocktail, Lee turned to the hickory-smoked bacon produced by Benton's, a celebrated American producer of cured meats. Grill four slices of smoked bacon to obtain 30ml (1fl oz) of hot fat. Pour this fat into a bottle of bourbon (first remove 50ml/1¾fl oz of spirits). Shake the bottle and leave to infuse at room temperature for 24 hours, then put in the freezer for two hours. The alcohol won't freeze but the fats will solidify. Strain the liquid into a clean bottle and voila! You've got a perfectly clear bourbon with a smoky bacon flavour.

This will make a dozen Benton's Old Fashioned. Bacon, maple syrup, bourbon: it will rejoice any Americanophile and goes well with barbecues or long winter evenings beside the fire (or the radiator). Nor did Don Lee stop there: he now gives seminars on the 'sensory neuroscience of cocktails' (sic) and develops bar utensils, such as spoons and shakers.

He is currently to be found at Boilermaker, formerly the Golden Cadillac in New York's East Village, where he makes good use of modern techniques such as juice clarification, centrifuges, and so on. Only the most experienced readers will follow in his footsteps.

PREPARATION

**Stir in a mixing glass**

TYPE OF GLASS

**Serve over ice cubes in an Old Fashioned glass**

PRESENTATION

**Garnish with a twist of orange peel**

DIFFICULTY

**Difficult**

STYLE

**Meaty, luscious cocktail**

TASTE

**Round and full-bodied, lightly spiced**

**FINISH**

**Bacon dominates, with a slight touch of smokiness**

# 12 Bijou

## INGREDIENTS

30ml (1fl oz) Aviation gin, 30ml (1fl oz) green Chartreuse, 30ml (1fl oz) red vermouth, 1 dash Orange bitters, lemon peel to serve (optional)

The first time I tasted this marvellous classic cocktail, I was told that it owed its name to the precious stones of which it was composed. The gin was the diamond; the vermouth, the ruby; the green Chartreuse was the emerald. I'm not the kind of person who looks a gift horse in the mouth and I don't question the stories I'm told overmuch, so long as the cocktail is good.

But thinking about it now, all that seems rather far-fetched. Why use the French word rather than 'jewel'? Perhaps because Bijou was a very popular name for theatres in the United States. In fact, there was a Bijou Theatre on Broadway in New York, precisely two blocks from the hotel where Harry Johnson, the bartender who popularized this recipe in his 1900 book, worked in 1898. And the name was certainly to be found in many provincial cities, including Cincinnati, where C.F. Lawlor worked; in 1895 he was the first to give this name to a slightly different and less original cocktail.

Johnson's Bijou is a good example of the cocktails of the first golden age, which had yet to abandon sweetness although the dry gin began to dominate. Here, unsurprisingly, it is associated with a sweet Italian vermouth. And, typical of the age, of course a liqueur could not be missed out. Very intelligently Johnson (or the anonymous inventor of this formula) chose green Chartreuse, the elixir made from 130 herbs, which marries perfectly with the gin and red vermouth and gives its full force and complexity to a mixture that, without it – or rather without it in such measure – would have resembled dozens of other cocktails of the era. Diamonds are forever whereas theatres close down (the Bijou in 1915). Perhaps that is why the first explanation of the name for this jewel of the mixologist's art is preferable.

**PREPARATION**

Stir in a mixing glass

**TYPE OF GLASS**

Serve in a cocktail glass

**PRESENTATION**

Garnish with a twist of lemon peel (optional)

**DIFFICULTY**

Moderate

**STYLE**

Sweet cocktail

**TASTE**

Sugary and very herby (pine)

FINISH

Lightly mentholated, spices and lemon

# 13 Blonde Bombshell

## INGREDIENTS

1 lemon, quartered,
6 mint leaves,
2 teaspoons sugar, 15ml
(½fl oz) vanilla syrup,
50ml (1¾fl oz) vanilla
vodka, 2 dashes lemon
bitters, 20ml (¾fl oz)
limoncello, mint sprig
and lemon slices to serve

I don't know which distiller was the first to produce flavoured vodka but it launched a huge market that includes a range from the aberrant to the absurd. But one mustn't sneer too much, for these products help to give your mixes a touch of flavour while retaining a neutral alcohol base, which makes life easier for the amateur as much as for the professional.

Of course lemon vodka wreaked havoc in the Cosmopolitan, the absolute classic of the 1980s that became a universal drinks icon in the 1990s, thanks to Madonna and the girls of *Sex in the City*. I prefer not to present it here – who needs another Cosmo? There is a better example of the judicious use of a flavoured vodka in an excellent cocktail created by Davy Nerambourg, which won him the 2007 Trophées du Bar, the industry's only independent competition in France.

The Blonde Bombshell is organized around vanilla and lemon, giving a flavour that has sometimes been described as being like a slice of lemon meringue pie. Muddle the first four ingredients in the glass (reserving one lemon slice to garnish). Next add the crushed ice, followed by the vodka and bitters, before stirring. Top up the glass with more crushed ice then pour the limoncello over. Lemon, vanilla, mint: it's a clear winner. It could have been too sweet, but this much-improved Caipiroska is totally balanced and all the more tasty if you use top-quality ingredients. Davy takes his Blonde Bombshell wherever he goes, most recently to Café Juliette, his bar in Lyons. But our deadly blonde can also be found on the menu of other French bars. Everywhere she goes she seduces male and female clients. It's the mark of a good cocktail – and of a good bartender.

PREPARATION

**Mix directly in an Old Fashioned glass**

PRESENTATION

**Serve over crushed ice, garnish with a sprig of mint and slices of lemon**

DIFFICULTY

**Difficult**

STYLE

**Rich, luscious cocktail**

TASTE

**Fresh and delicious, over the lemon and mint**

FINISH

**Short and sweet**

# 14 Blood & Sand

40ml (1¼fl oz) Scotch whisky, 20ml (¾fl oz) vermouth, 20ml (¾fl oz) Cherry Heering, 20ml (¾fl oz) orange juice, orange peel to serve (optional)

Two sweeping assertions: firstly, Scotch whisky and cocktails do not go well together; secondly, cocktails named after films or plays are often better than the works in question. Blood & Sand gives the lie to one of these pronouncements and confirms the other. Which is which depends on whether you like this cocktail or not!

Released in 1922, *Blood and Sand* was one of the legendary Rudolph Valentino's greatest successes. The Latin lover par excellence played the role of a matador whose blood would flow in the sand. When Valentino died four years later, a hundred thousand people came to pay a last tribute that turned into chaos: riot, vandalism and the intervention of mounted police. It's even said that despairing fans killed themselves. Fate is particularly cruel: nowadays practically nobody is desperate enough to see Valentino's films. Not one of them is considered a classic of the silent era (although personally I'm quite fond of *The Four Horsemen of the Apocalypse*). The cocktail named after this film appeared for the first time in 1930 in a book published in London (just to remind you, the US had been dry since the 1920s). It's not known precisely when and where it was invented, but I would not put too much faith in stories that suggest it's a Prohibition cocktail.

In any case, even if the situation has changed today, at the time there were few good cocktails made with Scotch (or orange juice). Despite featuring ingredients that do not, in theory, go together, not to mention strange proportions, the Blood & Sand gets the job done. It is the perfect mixture for those strange souls who crave the aromas of whisky without its alcoholic kick, plus a bit of fruit to boot. My wife's aunt adores it, and takes off if I suggest anything else. Good to know.

**PREPARATION**

Shake in a cocktail shaker

**TYPE OF GLASS**

Serve in a wine glass

**PRESENTATION**

Garnish with a twist of orange peel (optional)

**DIFFICULTY**

Moderate

**STYLE**

A fruity, whisky-flavoured cocktail

**TASTE**

Full and refreshing, cherry and vanilla to the fore

**FINISH**

Whisky, with a slightly bitter tang

# Bloody Mary

### INGREDIENTS

50ml (1¾fl oz) vodka,
2 teaspoons lemon
juice, 15ml (½fl oz)
tomato juice, 2 drops
Worcestershire sauce,
2 drops Tabasco,
2 pinches celery salt,
1 pinch black pepper,
½ teaspoon mustard,
celery stick to serve

There are three cocktails in this book that allegedly were invented in Harry's New York Bar in Paris but probably, in fact, were not. We could have included more, but that's not the point. Take the Bloody Mary, clearly the best known of all of them. It's supposed to have been created by Fernand Petiot at Harry's in 1921, although the bar wasn't officially labelled 'Harry's' until 1923.

Harry MacElhone did not publish the recipe in any of his books. The first mention of the cocktail dates from 1939, in the US. Suffice to add that canned tomato juice was not available commercially until 1928, a time when alcohol-free cocktail recipes that closely resembled the Bloody Mary began to make an appearance. Who knows, perhaps the inventor was not a bartender but a poor bloke who wanted to drink alcohol without it being noticed and had therefore added to his 'Tomato Cocktail' an odourless, insipid alcohol, vodka, which was only then beginning to reach the United States? Petiot or not, Paris or New York, will we ever get to the bottom of it? Anyway, we're ready to bet that the success of the Bloody Mary is largely due to the discreet nature of the spirit: drink early, with no bad breath.

During the 1950s, Hemingway, whose doctor (an optimist) had forbidden him to drink, drank Bloody Marys to fool his wife. That was at the Paris Ritz. Maybe he even believed that they were good for his health – such a lot of vitamins! Unsurprisingly, over time the Bloody Mary was transformed into the mandatory drink to accompany a proper brunch.

The Bloody Mary derives its character from the seasoning, which you can prepare to your liking. If you want a stronger taste of spirits, go for gin (this is called a Red Snapper) or tequila (in which case add spices used in Mexican cooking).

**PREPARATION**

**Mix directly in a Collins glass, serve over ice cubes**

**PRESENTATION**

**Garnish with a stick of celery**

**DIFFICULTY**

**Moderate**

**STYLE**

**The brunch cocktail**

**TASTE**

**Dense, slightly piquant and acidulated**

**FINISH**

**Salty and briny, tomatoes and spices**

# 16
# Blue Hawaii

INGREDIENTS

30ml (1fl oz) Puerto
Rican rum, 30ml
(1fl oz) vodka, 15ml
(½fl oz) sugar syrup,
15ml (½fl oz) lemon
juice, 15ml (½fl oz)
blue curaçao, 90ml
(3fl oz) pineapple juice,
pineapple wedge and
1 cherry to serve

You will keep reading that the art of the cocktail was in decline from the 1960s to the 1990s. In fact this decline can be easily traced, beginning precisely on the day when some wise guy decided that a blue cocktail was a good idea. Created in 1957 in Waikiki, the Blue Hawaii was so popular that it gave its name to a monument of tropical kitsch, one of Elvis Presley's biggest movie hits. It was not the first blue cocktail (one already existed in the 1930s, a far more glorious era) but we offer it as a dubious case in point, and all the more since it contains vodka, another great evil of the age when the US, seduced by the technical prowess of culinary modernity, seemed to have made an industrial choice of 'less flavour'.

Frankly, the problem lies not with the famous blue curaçao (technically the flavour is the same as in normal curaçao, although nobody would rank 'funny' colours among the best products of the category). The real concern with the Blue Hawaii is the lack of any spirit of character to offset the orgy of ingredients it offers. The vodka delivers alcohol and nothing else. But what about the rum?

Oh, come on. This is a vodka that is being passed off as a rum. The pineapple juice is definitely canned, while the lemon juice and sugar were bought ready mixed. Clearly the Blue Hawaii sums up all the problems of American gastronomy of the 1960s: artificial, insipid, utilitarian. Chinese takeaway, baseball on the black-and-white TV, dad home from Madison Avenue. Yummy. But the Blue Hawaii is visually one of the prettiest cocktails in this book. Don't tell my parents, they think I've got good taste.

**PREPARATION**

**Shake in a cocktail shaker**

**TYPE OF GLASS**

**Serve in a Hurricane or Collins glass**

**PRESENTATION**

**Garnish with a wedge of pineapple and a cherry**

**DIFFICULTY**

**Moderate**

**STYLE**

**Tropical blue cocktail**

**TASTE**

**Platform for the pineapple**

**FINISH**

**Short and simple**

# 17 Boulevardier

INGREDIENTS

45ml (1½fl oz) bourbon,
20ml (¾fl oz) red
vermouth, 20ml (¾fl oz)
Campari, 1 maraschino
cherry or orange peel
to serve

You often hear of the lost generation of Ernest Hemingway, F. Scott Fitzgerald and Gertrude Stein and of their passion for Paris in the 1920s. Given some of these writers' fondness for alcohol, it's clear that the appeal of Paris was not exclusively cultural, especially in an era when bars were illegal back home and securing a good drink was extremely complicated, even with lots of money. The city of light was one of the first in Europe to welcome the cocktail and Americans had long been enamoured of her charms. This only intensified after WW1 and the American community created a little microcosm in the city with its own bookshops, clubs, bars and ... magazines.

In 1927, journalists Arthur Moss and Erskine Gwynne founded *Boulevardier*, a magazine modelled on the *New Yorker*. Contributors included not only Hemingway but also Sinclair Lewis and Noël Coward (each undoubtedly deserves his own chapter in a book about drink and literature – there's already one about Hemingway alone). It's no surprise to learn in the second book by Harry MacElhone, boss of Harry's Bar, headquarters then and now of Americans in Paris, that Gwynne invented this recipe to celebrate the launch of the magazine.

Clearly the man had good taste: it's not only a fabulous cocktail but also ahead of its time. It's often presented as a Negroni with bourbon rather than gin. As we'll see, legend has it that the Negroni was created in 1921, but no recipe dating from that era has been found. So perhaps we should turn things around and claim the Boulevardier as a pioneer, even though the proportions and the way of serving it have changed? In any event, Campari, which already had a venerable history, was not used in cocktails until the 1920s. It soon found its classic recipe.

**PREPARATION**

Stir in a mixing glass

**TYPE OF GLASS**

Serve in a cocktail glass

**PRESENTATION**

Garnish with a maraschino cherry or a twist of orange peel

**DIFFICULTY**

Moderate

**STYLE**

Complex aperitif

**TASTE**

Bitter oranges, clove and cinnamon

**FINISH**

Lingering bitterness and vanilla notes

# 18 Bramble

## INGREDIENTS

60ml (2fl oz) gin, 30ml
(1fl oz) lemon juice, 15ml
(½fl oz) sugar syrup,
15ml (½fl oz) Merlet
Crème de mûre, lemon
slice to serve

No bartender in the UK is more respected than Dick Bradsell. He's been wielding shakers for over thirty years and, unlike many other figures in the business, he's never abandoned the bar to focus on consultancy or to present himself as a guru. And you'll still find him behind the bar on your next visit to London (you just need to know where ...).

Aside from his great experience, Bradsell's reputation is due to the impact he's had on the London cocktail scene. Mentor to all the bartenders who have put London on the map for the past fifteen years, in the 1990s he was one of the first to use (return to) fresh fruit and to think in terms of quality. The number of important bars he has launched is impossible to count. His influence radiates well beyond the UK: if the bartender in your favourite bar takes five minutes to make his Old Fashioned, it's because he is following the Bradsell method. Bradsell's cocktails are certainly worth a detour. The Espresso Martini, of course, but also the Bramble, an instant classic that has given its name to the best bar in Edinburgh (and the best European bar of the last four years, if one can believe the Top 50 published annually by the magazine *Drinks International*).

Created at Fred's Bar in 1984, like all classics the Bramble is very simple: gin, lemon juice, sugar syrup, shaken and served over crushed ice. The touch that changes everything is the drizzle of Crème de mûre over the cocktail. Not only does this distinguish it visually but it will also impress your guests – even though it's a perfectly simple manoeuvre. It's delicious, it takes no time at all and quality Crème de mûre is readily available. What are you waiting for?

**PREPARATION**

**Shake in a cocktail shaker (except for the Crème de mûre)**

**TYPE OF GLASS**

**Serve in an Old Fashioned glass**

**PRESENTATION**

**Garnish with a slice of lemon**

**DIFFICULTY**

**Moderate**

**STYLE**

**Refreshing cocktail**

**TASTE**

**Perfect balance between sweetness and tartness**

**FINISH**

**Tangy and fruity**

# 19

# Brandy Alexander

INGREDIENTS

30ml (1fl oz) cognac,
30ml (1fl oz) Crème de
cacao (brown), 30ml
(1fl oz) fresh cream or
crème fraîche, grated
nutmeg to serve

You sometimes read that what someone drinks says a lot about them as a person. I would add that it also says a lot about what we want others to think of us. And watch out for blunders: take the case of Peggy Olson at the end of the first season of *Mad Men*, a series largely set in the world of American advertising at the end of the 1950s. Peggy, who starts out as a secretary, begins to make her own merry way in this macho world and becomes the first woman to work in the creative department of her agency. On a blind date she tries to impress a young man by showing that she is a true modern, metropolitan woman and nobody's fool. She orders a Brandy Alexander before the meal.

Two-fold problem: it's a digestif, not an aperitif; it's a sugary cocktail that is often thought of (clichés die hard) as feminine. When Peggy tastes it, she makes another blunder: she grimaces. It's too strong. She shows us that she has made a random choice (this won't be the case with you) and, above all, that she is not yet ready to enter this macho world peopled with big drinkers, because she doesn't yet know the codes. Of course, the Brooklyn bumpkin who's not yet up to speed with the person she's going to share a meal (but nothing else) with, doesn't know it, but the viewer does.

The series scriptwriters display a subtle understanding of the social significance of one's choice of cocktail. And, indirectly, they send us an important message: whether we drink cocktails to be sophisticated or because we like them, each cocktail has its moment. Don't drink a Dry Martini at five in the morning or a Piña Colada as an aperitif! Brandy Alexander can be made with either cognac or Spanish brandy (which will be even more sugary). Made with gin you get a drier Alexander, but one equally good as 'dessert'.

**PREPARATION**

**Shake in a cocktail shaker**

**TYPE OF GLASS**

**Serve in a cocktail glass**

**PRESENTATION**

**Garnish with fresh nutmeg**

**DIFFICULTY**

**Moderate**

**STYLE**

**Chocolatey digestif**

**TASTE**

**Creamy and sugary**

**FINISH**

**Medium chocolate and spicy notes**

# Brandy Crusta

**INGREDIENTS**

60ml (2fl oz) Ferrand
1840 cognac, 1 teaspoon
lemon juice, 1 teaspoon
sugar syrup, ½ teaspoon
Ferrand Dry Curaçao,
2 dashes Angostura
bitters, lemon peel and
sugar to serve

New Orleans, before the American Civil War. The rotunda of the St Louis Hotel is a gigantic auction house where everything is for sale – the cotton, as well as the men and women who produce it. It is Louisiana's principal slave market. Behind the bar of this magnificent and nauseating establishment, Joseph Santini, an Italian emigrant, probably from Trieste, is busy quenching the thirst of a South that will soon disappear. And, although you wouldn't think it, he is revolutionizing the art of the cocktail. While he subsequently became a successful businessman and a prominent public figure, he is remembered today thanks to a small amount of lemon juice and a big sense of style that his predecessors lacked.

You see, Santini probably kept two things in mind: firstly, New Orleans is too hot and humid to be satisfied with a cocktail in its classic form (an Old Fashioned, basically) and secondly, something eye-catching sells better than something discreet (I hope that he didn't learn that in the rotunda). So he presented his drink in a small sugar-frosted wine glass, in which he placed the skin of a whole lemon. For his ingredients, he chose cognac (it's Creole country, after all), sugar, bitters and a little curaçao. So far this is just a sophisticated cocktail (other types of mixtures had other names). However, he added a touch of lemon. It may not seem much but the result was a whole new ball game: the watertight walls that separated the families of mixed drinks began to shatter. A few years later, vermouth hit America and everything was turned upside down, for good. But that's another story .... For the moment, be satisfied with drinking a Crusta. Jerry Thomas, who recorded the recipe in the first cocktail book in 1862, warns: inevitably, the Crusta will put a smile on your face.

**PREPARATION**

Stir in a mixing glass

**TYPE OF GLASS**

Serve in a small wine glass frosted with sugar (see page 218)

**PRESENTATION**

Garnish with the peel of a whole lemon

**DIFFICULTY**

Difficult

**STYLE**

Old Fashioned with lemon

**TASTE**

Round and rich, with a light freshness

**FINISH**

Orange to the fore, with spicy notes of clove and cinnamon

# Breakfast Martini

## INGREDIENTS

50ml (1¾fl oz) gin,
15ml (½fl oz) Cointreau,
15ml (½fl oz) lemon
juice, 1 teaspoon orange
marmalade, orange peel
to serve (optional)

During the 1940s, the V-shaped glass became the vessel of choice for the divine liquid that is the Martini. It even took its name. Gradually every cocktail served in a martini glass became a Martini, regardless of its ingredients. It's a curious example of transubstantiation, which we don't like and recommend that every drinker with good taste forgets. Of all these new Martinis, 99 per cent or more should be poured straight down the sink.

However, some have managed to establish themselves and since we're not priggish we include three in this book. As its name indicates, the Breakfast Martini presents itself as the first drink of the day, although the most scrupulous among you may prefer to take it with brunch. The great discovery of its creator, Salvatore Calabrese, an Italian who moved to London more than thirty years ago and who modestly calls himself The Maestro, is to sweeten the mixture with marmalade.

Was this really a major discovery? Perhaps not: those with long memories point out that Harry Craddock, bartender at the Savoy's legendary American Bar in the 1930s, suggested a Marmalade Cocktail of gin, lemon juice and orange marmalade, in his book. Was Calabrese, who's not just anybody, inspired by Craddock's recipe (he wasn't the first), or was it more a case of great minds (or should I say egos) think alike? At all events, he adds Cointreau, to accentuate the orange and balance the cocktail.

The result is a small gem of a drink to which the bitter orange flavour of the liqueur and the marmalade bring a complexity that a simple syrup could never deliver, not to mention the texture. This is a cocktail that should be drunk as early as your religion allows. I have scientifically determined that this is possible from 10.40am onwards (an old story). Shake well to dissolve the marmalade.

**PREPARATION**

**Shake in a cocktail shaker**

**TYPE OF GLASS**

**Serve in a Martini glass**

**PRESENTATION**

**Garnish with a twist of orange peel (optional)**

**DIFFICULTY**

**Difficult**

**STYLE**

**'Martini' for brunch**

**TASTE**

**Round and lively**

FINISH

Short, citrussy, slightly bitter

# 22

# Cameron's Kick

## INGREDIENTS

30ml (1fl oz) Irish whiskey, 30ml (1fl oz) Scotch whisky, 20ml (¾fl oz) lemon juice, 20ml (¾fl oz) almond (orgeat) syrup, lemon peel to serve

If there aren't many cocktails made with Scotch whisky, what is the deal with Irish whiskey? True, the situation is changing, albeit slowly. For now, finding a classic is like searching for a needle in a haystack. I'm very fond of the Tipperary, a sort of Irish Manhattan with a little green Chartreuse, sugar syrup and orange bitters. But it's rather similar to several cocktails mentioned in these pages. So what to choose then? It's a real puzzler.

However, with a dash of perseverance, one can unearth an excellent cocktail that really pushes the envelope: it contains both Scotch whisky and Irish whiskey. Magnificent. And, although he didn't claim paternity, it may have been invented by a Scot, Harry MacElhone. Whatever the case, he published the first recipe in 1922. Not content with bringing together two whisk(e)ys that popular wisdom tends – I don't know why – to consider bad bases for a cocktail, he adds orgeat.

On paper at least, Cameron's Kick is decidedly a very strange cocktail. But it is a recipe of its time. During the 1920s, the European cocktail was characterized by two things: a strong tendency to play with the formula of the perfect Martini (dry and sweet vermouth in equal parts) and/or the creation of improbable, experimental mixtures that were a great deal more avant-garde than the American output of the previous twenty years. For example, the first printed recipe for a tequila-based cocktail (the Picador, a Margarita that dared not speak its name) was to be found in Europe. The oddities often missed the mark (as books published during this period can testify), whereas others miraculously worked. This is the case with Cameron's Kick, a 'quiet', soothing drink that nonetheless demands to be drunk again and again, but in moderation. Squaring the circle.

**PREPARATION**

Shake in a cocktail shaker

**TYPE OF GLASS**

Serve in a Martini glass

**PRESENTATION**

Garnish with a twist of lemon peel

**DIFFICULTY**

Moderate

**STYLE**

Complex 'sour' cocktail

**TASTE**

Lightly spicy and sour

**FINISH**

Delicate, floral, with walnut and lemon notes

# 23 Casse Noisette (Nutcracker)

INGREDIENTS

30ml (1fl oz) vodka,
30ml (1fl oz) coffee
liqueur, 30ml (1fl oz)
hazelnut syrup, 40ml
(1¼fl oz) single cream,
chocolate shavings to
serve (optional)

One of the first rules a good bartender should learn is that the best recipe is nothing without a name that does it full justice. In 2001 when Julien Escot created this cocktail, at the bar of the Hotel du Cap-Eden Roc, Antibes, no doubt he had Tchaikovsky's ballet in mind, which would surely have pleased his exclusive clientele. For others, of course, something else might come to mind. This ambiguity might have caused a problem, but if you ask, Julien will tell you that of all his cocktails it is the Nutcracker that has undoubtedly made the biggest impact.

Julien is one of the great French bartenders. He has worked in many countries, garnered many prestigious awards and has managed to get his bar, the Papa Doble, onto the list of the world's 50 best bars, even though it is based in a provincial city (Montpellier), far from all centres of influence. He has also created some excellent cocktail recipes, which are sometimes very sophisticated and therefore too complicated for an amateur to recreate.

But from the Nutcracker to the creations that feature on the Papa Doble's latest menu, it is all about flavour. Why have I chosen the Nutcracker rather than another cocktail? Because, in addition to its undeniable gustatory quality and relative ease of preparation, it represents a notable moment in the evolution of the cocktail. One cannot suddenly jump from the artificialities of the 1980s to the Japanese whisky of the 2010s. The cocktail first had to be revived with whatever came to hand, taking ingredients that were in fashion – in this case, vodka and liqueurs – and bringing them to a balanced whole. The Nutcracker demonstrates that this process took place not only in London (Espresso Martini), but also, to some extent, in France. And, often, in hotels. Who'd have thought it…?

**PREPARATION**

**Shake in a cocktail shaker (except for the single cream)**

**TYPE OF GLASS**

**Serve in a Martini glass; shake the single cream in a cocktail shaker without ice, then pour over the cocktail, garnish with chocolate shavings (optional)**

**PRESENTATION**

**Garnish with bitter cocoa powder**

**DIFFICULTY**

**Difficult**

**STYLE**

**Digestif cocktail**

**TASTE**

**Velvety and rich**

**FINISH**

**Medium and round, hazelnut and coffee notes**

# 24 La Chaparra

INGREDIENTS
.......................................................
45ml (1½fl oz) Havana
Club 3 Años, 15ml
(½fl oz) red vermouth,
1 teaspoon sugar syrup,
peel of 1 lime plus extra
to serve

There are some obvious ways of giving a cocktail a lime flavour: use juice or cordial, or flavour the surface of your drink with the zest of lime peel. In the 1930s the Cubans came up with another solution that gives the cocktail the benefit of the freshness of lime without diluting it. Many cocktails served in the famous El Floridita in Havana used this method, including the bar's adaptation of the Old Fashioned or the Manhattan (the Floridita Special). And what exactly did it involve? Whether shaken or stirred, the drinks were made with the peel of an entire lime.

The best example is La Chaparra, a cocktail that might have been a simple, slightly sweet Cuban Manhattan. But by adding the peel of a lime to the bottom of the mixing glass and muddling it lightly in the syrup, before adding the other ingredients, ice and then stirring, the drink is completely transformed. The lime brings a tinge of acidity and bitterness as well as a great sensation of freshness. The cocktail, however, remains as strong as if it were almost 100 per cent alcohol. If you had discovered this cocktail without knowing how it was made, it would seem like a miracle. And behold – the technique is actually easy, but it's one that, sadly, nobody now seems to use (a word to the wise).

I urge you to compare this recipe both with and without the little lime peel trick. Discover the difference it makes, and learn all the subtlety, the ingenuity and the talent of the Cuban school. A *chaparra* is also Latin slang for a 'small woman' and was the name of the biggest sugar plantation in Cuba, too. American-owned, it was managed by a Cuban engineer called Mario Menocal, who became president of the Republic from 1913–21. His election inspired the creation of the famous Presidente.

PREPARATION

**Shake in a cocktail shaker**

TYPE OF GLASS

**Serve in a cocktail glass**

PRESENTATION

**Garnish with lime peel**

DIFFICULTY

**Difficult**

STYLE

**Cuban aperitif**

TASTE

**Light, a touch of acidity with molasses notes**

**FINISH**

Initially more sugary, lightly spiced and herby, then the acidity returns

# 25 Chartreuse Swizzle

## INGREDIENTS

45ml (1½fl oz) green Chartreuse, 30ml (1fl oz) pineapple juice, 20ml (¾fl oz) lime juice, 15ml (½fl oz) Falernum, mint sprig to serve

For the meaning of the word swizzle and the technique involved, wait until the magnificent Queen's Park Swizzle (*see* page 164). I prefer to dedicate this entry to the art of flavour associations. Basic stuff, I hear you say. We know that rum and lime go well together; that cognac and Peychaud's bitters have a particular affinity, that a simple twist of lemon will give a lift to a mixture of gin and dry vermouth. Consequently, everyone ends up playing with the same combinations. Or perhaps some wise guys reflect on the specifics of each product. For example, Tanqueray Ten gin is made with camomile and grapefruit. The professional observer quickly tires of seeing 'creative' bartenders wearing out this particular partnership. The palate becomes fatigued and ends up rejecting good but somewhat dull mixtures.

Happily, some flavour alliances continue to surprise. Does green Chartreuse and pineapple sound like a magical couple? Marco Dionysos, who invented the Chartreuse Swizzle in 2003, realized its potential. It's a truly magnificent match and not yet well known. In all honesty, and as the journalist Gaylor Olivier has noted, in 1888 there was already a cocktail known as the Brandy Fix, made with pineapple syrup and Chartreuse, while the Swamp Water, used during the 1970s to promote Chartreuse by US importers of the liqueur, lacked just one ingredient for it to be the Swizzle's twin brother. It's the eternal question: is your bartender genuinely very creative or might he have found his inspiration in a long-forgotten recipe? We'll let them off lightly: it's not so important as long as it excites the taste buds. And Dionysos knew how to tickle them with a forgotten combination; at least he hasn't tried to make a strawberry Daiquiri with balsamic vinegar.

**PREPARATION**

Mix in a Collins glass, serve over crushed ice

**PRESENTATION**

Garnish with a sprig of mint, drink through a straw

**DIFFICULTY**

Difficult

**STYLE**

Complex tropical cocktail

**TASTE**

Ample, tangy, ginger notes

**FINISH**

Medium. Herbs (oregano, mint) and pineapple

# 26

# Clover Club

### INGREDIENTS

50ml (1¾ fl oz) gin, 30ml
(1 fl oz) lemon juice,
15ml (½ fl oz) Merlet
Crème de framboise,
2 teaspoons sugar syrup,
egg white, raspberries
to serve

One of the most neglected branches in the art of drinking is the evolution of target audiences for a particular drink. Take the Clover Club, a slightly sugary, rose-coloured cocktail tasting of raspberries: an ideal alternative to offer a woman instead of the Cosmopolitan. And yet ...! According to David Wondrich, member emeritus of the (cocktail) Academy, during the years of its greatest popularity (around 1910), the Clover Club was a cocktail for men. After all, it's the house drink of a club of the same name, which is reserved for Philadelphia captains of industry and other notables. And to think that during the same era women drank ... Martinis!

It's almost a reversal of gender stereotypes. For instance, in an educational context: when did pink become a colour for little girls and when did a stiff Martini become a symbol of middle-class masculinity? But enough of politics (sexual or otherwise): the essential thing is what's in our glass. You will have recognized (yet again!) the Gin Sour formula, but this time the syrup is replaced by an excellent raspberry liqueur.

Delicious! Of course this cocktail can also be made with raspberry syrup, but in that case it's important to use a quality brand (or make it yourself; it's not difficult and even frozen fruit works well).

Personally I drink lots of Clover Club when raspberries are in season (from June to September). This involves putting six fresh, ripe raspberries in the shaker and adding an appropriate amount of sugar syrup (around 20ml/¾fl oz, depending on the acidity of the berries). Muddle, and then add the other ingredients. You'll see, the colour is splendid and the taste deeply satisfying, whether you are a 21st-century man or a 1910 woman.

PREPARATION

**Shake in a cocktail shaker**

TYPE OF GLASS

**Serve in a cocktail glass**

PRESENTATION

**Garnish with raspberries**

DIFFICULTY

**Difficult**

STYLE

**Delicious aperitif**

TASTE

**Silky, tangy but delicious**

**FINISH**

**Medium, raspberry coulis or sorbet**

# 27

## Corpse Reviver #2

### INGREDIENTS

30ml (1fl oz) Aviation
gin, 30ml (1fl oz) Lillet,
30ml (1fl oz) Cointreau,
30ml (1fl oz) lemon juice,
2 drops Pernod absinthe,
lemon peel or star anise
to serve

I repeat: alcohol abuse is dangerous to health. But let's be realistic: there are days when we let go and indulge a bit. The following day, there's often a heavy price to pay. And in times when hygiene was less important, bartenders around the world often played pharmacist; instead of an aspirin they would suggest a whole range of drinks to get the poor customer back on his feet in time for the first meeting of the morning. But why settle for waking up a scrambled brain when we can 'revive a corpse'?

The Corpse Reviver was born around the middle of the 19th century, although to look at the original recipe, you might wonder why it's so called: it's a cocktail like any other, although possibly less good, that mixes cognac, calvados and vermouth without a single ingredient that might kick-start a battered body attempting to recover the morning after. However, it seems to have proved its effectiveness as it has spawned sequels. Since we're not talking movies here, the best is definitely the #2, created by Harry Craddock at London's Savoy Hotel in the 1920s. It's the perfect blockbuster, easy to make (equal parts gin, lemon juice, Lillet and Cointreau, completed by two drops of absinthe), simple looking but complex enough to tickle your numb brain.

Absinthe was never illegal in the UK and Craddock used it until his French stock ran out. In this recipe the green fairy is the little touch that, together with the bitterness of the (Kina) Lillet of the time, whispered in the corpse's ear that it was time to rejoin the land of the living. But be careful: Craddock, who undoubtedly had more sense than the saloon bartenders of the American West, bluntly stated 'four of these taken in swift succession will un-revive the corpse again'. You have been warned.

**PREPARATION**

**Shake in a cocktail shaker**

**TYPE OF GLASS**

**Serve in a cocktail glass**

**PRESENTATION**

**Garnish with a twist of lemon peel or a star anise**

**DIFFICULTY**

**Moderate**

**STYLE**

**Morning-after cocktail**

**TASTE**

**Tangy, lots of citrus balanced by the gin**

**FINISH**

**Lingering aniseed, herby yet always a touch of acidity**

# 28 Daiquiri

INGREDIENTS

60ml (2fl oz) Havana
Club 3 Años, 30ml (1fl oz)
lime juice, 15ml (½fl oz)
sugar syrup, lime peel
to serve

You've probably already tried a strawberry, banana or mango Daiquiri. Forget those and concentrate on what the Cubans call the Daiquiri Natural, allegedly invented by Jennings Cox, an American mining engineer who worked near Santiago. As the recipe's three ingredients (light rum, sugar, lime) are the most common on the island, some think that this typically Cuban mixture predates by many years the mass arrival of the Yankees after the Spanish-American war of 1898. Others correctly point out that since it's prepared in a shaker and served as a short drink without ice it follows the American method.

In fact the Daiquiri was born shortly before 1910 from the meeting of two cultures: the increasingly numerous US tourists and the Cuban *cantinero*. During the 1920s it conquered the world. In the 1930s, Constante Ribalaigua, legendary bartender of Havana's El Floridita, innovated, preparing it in a blender and giving it little brothers (Numbers 2, 3 and 4) under the astonished gaze of Hemingway, who did so much to make this bar (and the cocktail) famous that it now has a statue of him.

The fathers of the Tiki or tropical cocktail that triumphed after World War II also learned everything from Constante: nearly all the classics of that school are 'Daiquiris squared or cubed', according to Beachbum Berry, the current specialist. This global popularity has an unfortunate consequence: the honourable Daiquiri is often badly made. There are a few ground rules to follow: always use a light and aromatic Cuban-style rum; freshly squeezed lime juice; half as much sugar as juice – the cocktail should be slightly sour. Prepared in a shaker or blender, the balance achieved, in your glass will be proof that there is sometimes nothing more perfect than absolute simplicity.

**PREPARATION**

**Mix in a cocktail shaker or a blender**

**TYPE OF GLASS**

**Serve in a cocktail glass**

**PRESENTATION**

**Garnish with a twist of lime peel**

**DIFFICULTY**

**Moderate**

**STYLE**

**The king of tropical cocktails**

**TASTE**

**Sugar cane and citrus**

**FINISH**

**The slight acidity cleanses the palate**

# Dark 'n' Stormy®

INGREDIENTS
......................

½ lime (in quarters),
60ml (2 fl oz) Gosling's
Black Seal rum, 100ml
(3½ fl oz) ginger beer,
lime wedge to serve

'It was a dark and stormy night'. This is the opening sentence, now much mocked, of an 1830 novel by Edward Bulwer-Lytton, a writer who has unwittingly given his name to a prize for 'the opening sentence to the worst of all possible novels'. We also owe to him 'the pen is mightier than the sword', incorrectly attributed to Richelieu. A link with the Dark 'n' Stormy®? Who knows ...? In any case, the drink's creation doubtless owes less to a scribbler than to English sailors who, being specialists in both the storm and alcohol departments, were true connoisseurs. The one surely helped them to survive the other. The Dark here is the sticky rum of Bermuda, where the cocktail has become the national drink (and where, Triangle or not, storms and tempests are not unknown). The Stormy is the ginger beer (with a ginger kick a lot stronger than ginger ale).

The combination is as simple as it is fabulous. In the US people like to add a little lime juice. And why not? There isn't a lot more to say about this recipe, whose origins remain very vague. However, there's another feature of the Dark 'n' Stormy®: it's one of the few cocktails to be trademarked. There's no question of marketing a Dark 'n' Stormy® with any other rum than Gosling's.

While the brand does not pursue bars that offer Jamaican rum, Gosling's stands firm in ensuring that nobody markets a can of Dark 'n' Stormy® with any product other than Gosling's rum, or promotes their own rum by using this recipe in its publicity. That does not mean that we cannot propose a recipe with the same ingredients, changing the rum (on the contrary: recipes cannot be trademarked), so one can promote a Martinique rum, for example, mixed with ginger beer, but under a different name.

**PREPARATION**

**Mix in a Collins glass**

**PRESENTATION**

**Serve over ice cubes, garnish with a wedge of lime**

**DIFFICULTY**

**Easy**

**STYLE**

**Refreshing yet powerful long drink**

**TASTE**

**Both heavy and refreshing, spicy**

**FINISH**

**Ginger and lots of molasses**

# 30 Death In The Afternoon

INGREDIENTS

30ml (1fl oz) Pernod
absinthe, 120ml (4fl oz)
Champagne

Bullfighting is not popular these days. Even in Spain, it is increasingly criticized and has been banned in Catalonia. So it's difficult to imagine a great contemporary literary figure displaying his admiration for the confrontation between man and bull. For those who don't come from the land of bulls, it is impossible to escape the mental images inspired by the works of Picasso. The artist was as fascinated by the aurochs depicted by the artists of the Lascaux caves as by the man in his 'suit of lights' emerging from the shadows to make his way across the sand of a bullring.

Hemingway, too, was never far away, number one in the pantheon of big-drinking writers who loved the *corrida*. And Hemingway's take is never more clearly displayed than in *Death in the Afternoon*, where he evokes the ritual aspects of the combat and draws a parallel with the artist's search for meaning. One cannot help wondering what linked the arenas of Madrid and Pamplona on a spring afternoon with Champagne and absinthe, since Hemingway composed a second 'Death in the afternoon': a cocktail that combines these two ingredients.

This was his contribution to *So Red the Nose*, a book wittily subtitled *Breath in the Afternoon*, a collection of recipes invented by celebrities. We know that Champagne is treacherous – and as for absinthe …! Nevertheless, Hemingway suggests that we should 'drink three to five of these, slowly'.

As a precaution I must emphasize that while Hemingway (often) had good taste, he didn't necessarily give good advice. As Philip Green, author of an excellent book on Hemingway and alcohol, reminds us, the editor of *So Red the Nose* added this rather useful clarification: 'Drink more than six glasses of this cocktail and … the sun also rises'.

PREPARATION

**Pour the absinthe into a Champagne flute, then gently top up with well-chilled Champagne**

DIFFICULTY

**Easy**

STYLE

**Aniseed Champagne**

TASTE

**Slight acidity, aniseed dominant**

FINISH

**Medium, the Champagne submerged by the herbal notes**

# 31 El Diablo

INGREDIENTS
.................................

45ml (1½fl oz) Excellia
tequila reposado 15ml
(½fl oz) Crème de cassis,
15ml (½fl oz) lime juice,
90ml (3fl oz) ginger
beer, lime wedge or
blackcurrent to serve

Despite the best efforts of its producers and importers, tequila continues to have a bad reputation, being too closely associated for many with the disenchantment felt in the early hours as the pale light of dawn crept over the student bar. I don't wish to lecture but I will just say this: make sure the label lists blanco (silver), reposado (cask-aged for at least two months) or añejo (aged for at least a year), and that your tequila is specified as 100 per cent agave.

Don't accept anything else, because it would mean that the product you are about to ingest contains no more than 51 per cent fermented agave distillate. Therefore the tequila has been cut, usually with a mixture of agave and cane sugar. It's cheaper, produced with less care and, above all, has less flavour: the agave takes up to ten years to reach maturity, and its flesh is baked to extract the juice that will ferment. Forewarned is forearmed.

Here we have two categories of drinkers: those who know a good Margarita and those who drink Tequila Sunrise. With El Diablo, we want to offer an alternative to drinkers of the latter, insipid mixture. It has the advantage of being simple to make and requires ingredients that are relatively easy to find. While everyone knows that tequila goes very well with lime, the professionals will tell you that grapefruit (*see* the Paloma, page 144) is also an ideal partner. The same goes for blackcurrant, although this is less well known. Trader Vic, emperor of the tropical cocktail, may have created this recipe after World War II. A last word of advice: if you can get ginger beer rather than ginger ale, your drink will gain in complexity and flavour. Regardless of which you go for, however, El Diablo is almost as simple to make as a Sunrise, is equally easy to drink, but is definitely streets ahead in quality.

**PREPARATION**

Mix directly in a Collins glass, serve over ice cubes

**PRESENTATION**

Garnish with a wedge of lime or a blackcurrant

**DIFFICULTY**

Moderate

**STYLE**

Refreshing long drink

**TASTE**

Tangy and spicy, with earthy notes

**FINISH**

Long, dominated by the ginger and jammy, berry fruit notes

# 32 Diplomat

45ml (1½fl oz)
La Quintinye dry
vermouth, 30ml
(1fl oz) La Quintinye red
vermouth, 20ml (¾fl oz)
maraschino liqueur,
2 dashes orange bitters,
orange peel to serve

More than thirty cocktails already! Time for a break. You won't find any alcohol-free recipes in this book, but all the same I do suggest a few fairly light cocktails (remember the Bamboo?). The Diplomat is one such, and not the least of those at the lighter end of the scale, even if few bartenders seem familiar with it (it's never too late to catch up). Diplomatic discretion applies: the creator of this recipe remains anonymous. Robert Vermeire, who published it for the first time in 1922, nevertheless clarified that it was 'very well-known in the French diplomatic service'. Where did he get this information? Hush-hush.

If Edward Snowden and WikiLeaks had existed at the time, we might have been able to get to the bottom of the story (not to mention many other cocktail stories). No such luck. In any case, it is obvious that it relates to a profession where it's best to keep a clear head. For high-level discussions, a Diplomat is better than a Sazerac. A perfidious spirit might remark that back in 1922 the war from which the diplomats had just emerged did not represent their finest hour. But let's not blame the cocktail .... Many amateurs hesitate to order drinks that do not feature spirits over 20 per cent. Perhaps in the belief that cocktail prices are justified only by their strength. Big mistake: you pay for a taste experience, preferably in a pleasant setting.

The complexity of vermouth, an aromatic fortified wine, should satisfy any demanding palate (not just those who want to hold back at the beginning or end of the evening). Here you find a mixture of lightly oxidized, dry French vermouth and sweeter Italian-style vermouth. Their herbaceous notes are reinforced by the maraschino (made with cherry stones, not the fruit), while the orange bitters transform the Diplomat into a true cocktail.

PREPARATION

**Stir in a mixing glass**

TYPE OF GLASS

**Serve in a Martini or cocktail glass**

PRESENTATION

**Garnish with a twist of orange peel**

DIFFICULTY

**Moderate**

STYLE

**Light aperitif**

TASTE

**Syrupy and herby, with a slight acidity**

**FINISH**

**Short, on the vanilla, orange and herbs**

# Douglas Fairbanks

## INGREDIENTS

60ml (2fl oz) gin, 30ml
(1fl oz) Merlet apricot
brandy, 30ml (1fl oz) lime
juice, egg white, lime
zest to serve (optional)

He was the king of Hollywood. He played Zorro, d'Artagnan, Robin Hood, he founded United Artists with Charlie Chaplin and, like everyone else, Douglas Fairbanks visited Cuba in the early 1920s, when the island was a haven of easy-living and good alcohol a stone's throw from the drought of the new American desert.

Accompanied by his wife, Mary Pickford, Fairbanks probably came across Fred Kaufman, a Brit who spoke English with a Spanish accent and hadn't waited for Prohibition to begin his island hopping. At the time Kaufman worked at the Sevilla-Biltmore, Havana's number one luxury hotel, built by Cubans and bought by Americans in 1919. Its Seville-inspired façade still awaits visitors on the magnificent Prado. If you have the opportunity, admire the view from the ballroom on the top floor where everyone from Josephine Baker to Al Capone danced, drank and dined.

According to several journalists of the time, Kaufman invented two cocktails for the most powerful couple of Hollywood's golden age. Mary's is still famous; Douglas' sank into oblivion. Nevertheless it is worth a detour, all the more because it proves that the Cuban school was not based solely on rum. Quite the contrary, it transpires. The Douglas Fairbanks is a bit scary when mixing it for the first time. More liqueur (apricot) than lime juice sets off a diabetes alarm in one's head. But fear not, it works; it's balanced and the strange alliance reveals the gin to be the ideal medium for celebrating an unusual marriage. If you add the egg white, you'll get a cocktail as silky as Douglas Fairbanks's moustache and just as charming as when, transformed into Robin Hood, he laid aside his bow to seduce Maid Marian.

PREPARATION

**Shake in a cocktail shaker**

TYPE OF GLASS

**Serve in a Martini or cocktail glass**

PRESENTATION

**Garnish with lime zest (optional)**

DIFFICULTY

**Difficult**

STYLE

**Unusual tropical cocktail**

TASTE

**Silky, controlled acidity, citrus and apricot**

**FINISH**

**Short, the apricot opens out over floral, slightly spicy notes**

# 34 Dry Martini

INGREDIENTS

50ml (1¾fl oz) gin, 20ml
(¾fl oz) dry vermouth,
1 dash orange bitters, 1
olive or lemon peel
to serve

The Dry Martini is the most elegant of cocktails. Just the shape of the glass evokes sophistication. Iconic cocktail, cocktail of icons: the Martini is Grace Kelly in Hitchcock movies, it's Bette Davis in *All About Eve*, it's James 'shaken, not stirred' Bond, it's filmmaker Luis Buñuel who dedicated a page of his memoirs to it. But why? Nothing could have foretold the successful result of the fortuitous meeting between a bottle of English gin and a French vermouth in an ordinary bar at the end of the 19th century.

Perhaps it owes its popularity to the transparency that lends it a sense of purity. Or maybe it's the beauty of its glass, whether you prefer the one to which it gave its name or the splendid Nick and Nora glasses (so-called after the bibulous protagonists of the 1934 film *The Thin Man*). Perhaps it was its innocent air when raised to the lips of a silent-screen diva? Or maybe the answer lies in the taste.

In fact this dry yet aromatic cocktail has the same impact on your taste buds as an Art Deco building has on your eyes. But I'm getting carried away. H.L. Mencken rightly considered it 'the only American invention as perfect as the sonnet', but beware its poetic airs. Dorothy Parker, who knew a thing or two about verse and small glasses, warns not to take more than two, at the risk of finding yourself under the table ... or under the host. However, there was no excess in her day: a Dry Martini was four measures of gin to one of vermouth. Churchill was satisfied with the gin alone. James Bond preferred his with vodka. Today a sad fate beckons: order a Martini and you risk being served with frozen ethanol. In this brutal world, it's high time to return to the genuine Dry Martini. Perhaps even to try the original version, published (in Paris) in 1904: half gin, half vermouth. Strong and delicate: a true delight.

**PREPARATION**

**Stir in a mixing glass**

**TYPE OF GLASS**

**Serve in a Martini glass**

**PRESENTATION**

**Garnish with an olive or a twist of lemon peel**

**DIFFICULTY**

**Moderate**

**STYLE**

**Dry, strong aperitif**

**TASTE**

**Silky and aromatic cocktail with dominating gin notes**

**FINISH**

**Long, with a slight acidity thanks to the vermouth**

# 35

# Earl Grey Mar-Tea-Ni

## INGREDIENTS

60ml (2fl oz) gin infused
with Earl Grey (see
right), 30ml (1fl oz) sugar
syrup, 30ml (1fl oz)
lemon juice, egg white,
lemon peel to serve

It's said that punch owes its name to the Indian word *panch*, meaning five, i.e. the number of ingredients necessary to make it: alcohol, citrus fruit, sugar, spice and water or tea. Tea. Now there's an ingredient that still remains strangely under-exploited by bartenders. And yet there are plenty of terrific applications, whether it is flavoured or not.

Lapsang souchong gives fabulous results, as does gunpowder green tea. It's wonderful, whether smoked or astringent, slightly lemony or spicy. Tea can stretch a long drink, make a syrup or a foam or be infused directly into spirits. This last method is the one chosen by Audrey Saunders, New York's high priestess of the cocktail, a former pupil of Dale DeGroff and owner of the cult bar Pegu Club, when, around the year 2000 she created an instant classic: the Earl Grey Mar-Tea-Ni.

She began by mixing the contents of a bottle of gin with four tablespoons of loose Earl Grey and left it to infuse for two hours at room temperature. It's important to use a good-quality tea, and personally I opt for an Earl Grey with a base of an excellent Yunnan black tea. You can of course reduce the quantities as necessary, so long as you keep the same proportions.

Once the liquor is strained (keep any leftovers in the refrigerator), you will have a gin whose spicy, citrussy notes go marvellously with the Earl Grey tannins and bergamots. Add sugar, lemon juice and egg white and the magic happens. Like the Breakfast Martini (*see* page 50) it's an ideal cocktail for an unconventional breakfast, or a High Tea without Champagne. 'Drink more tea' therefore doesn't exclude another motto: 'drink more gin'. And to think that it was not an Englishwoman but an American who made this discovery. What a shock!

PREPARATION

**Shake in a cocktail shaker**

TYPE OF GLASS

**Serve in a cocktail glass**

PRESENTATION

**Garnish with a twist of lemon peel**

DIFFICULTY

**Difficult**

STYLE

**Teatime cocktail**

TASTE

**Silky, round, citrus and tea notes**

**FINISH**

Gourmand, lightly tannic

# 36 Espresso Martini

## INGREDIENTS

60ml (2fl oz) vodka,
40ml (1¼fl oz) espresso,
15ml (½fl oz) sugar
syrup, 1 teaspoon
Kahlua, coffee beans
to serve

Oddly enough, in music, as in the cinema and even in fashion (yes, really!), the 1980s are seen in a much better light today than they were ten years ago, but in terms of fashionable cocktails the leading products of the 1980s don't get a look in. Bars with no vodka, cranberry juice scorned, Midori viewed with contempt. However, it wasn't all bad and this cocktail is living proof.

The Espresso Martini was created by Dick Bradsell in the 1980s for a model who came into the bar asking for something to 'wake me up, and then f**k me up'. So it was not the soberest decade, nor the classiest. We can thank Bradsell for staying stylish despite the circumstances. It's no surprise to learn that the base spirit is vodka, to which is added an espresso freshly brewed using the best possible coffee, and sugar. To reinforce the coffee notes as well as the cocktail's strength, Bradsell turned to Kahlua, a Mexican coffee liqueur that has also lost favour with smart, fashionable bartenders. If the latter deign to make this cocktail, they will choose a house liqueur or a product like Galliano Ristretto, which is actually quite commendable.

Of course, coffee, sugar and vodka do not make the most complex of cocktails (and consequently I urge you to use the best possible espresso, as the balance of the drink depends upon it). But simple needn't mean bad either; it's perfectly well constructed and wakes you up. First job done. As for getting smashed, we've come across a lot worse since then and along with the inclusion of the cocktail in this book comes my earnest advice for responsible consumption. After that, you can ignore me if you wish; I won't tell you how to behave, so long as you don't do it to the sound of Adam & the Ants.

**PREPARATION**

**Shake in a cocktail shaker**

**TYPE OF GLASS**

**Serve in a Martini glass**

**PRESENTATION**

**Garnish with three coffee beans**

**DIFFICULTY**

**Difficult**

**STYLE**

**Anti-grogginess cocktail**

**TASTE**

**Gentle entry, followed by roasted notes**

**FINISH**

The bitterness of the coffee soothed by notes of vanilla

# 37 Fog Cutter

## INGREDIENTS

60ml (2fl oz) Cuban rum,
30ml (1fl oz) cognac,
15ml (½fl oz) gin, 60ml
(2fl oz) lemon juice, 30ml
(1fl oz) orange juice, 15ml
(½fl oz) orgeat (almond)
syrup, 15ml (½fl oz)
cream sherry, mint sprig
to serve

Is there a hint of irony here? Can such a strong cocktail really help pierce the fog? Didn't its creator, Trader Vic, say that after the second you would no longer be able to see the fog anyway? The Fog Cutter is the Long Island Iced Tea of cocktail lovers. Some say it is the source of greater damage than pleasure.

It is still worth considering, though, because it demonstrates two things: that the Tiki cocktail, invented by Vic and his rival Don the Beachcomber, was made not only with rum and that the formula always stayed the same. So what is the Tiki cocktail? A Cinemascope version of a Caribbean cocktail (like a Daiquiri or Planter's Punch). Why settle for one spirit when you can have three (in this case, brandy, gin and rum)? Why enjoy just one juice when you can add several? And why make the syrup simple when you can add an unlimited number of flavours? It's a balancing act and one that doesn't always work.

The setting in which it was drunk – exotica playing in the background, bamboo on the walls, flowered shirts, Polynesian glasses and not one window to the outside world – was a bolt-hole ('help me forget the Soviets, the bomb and the old lady'). There was something fascinating about it, even over the top, a sense of being larger than life (and certainly more exciting), which made you prepared to soon forgive certain shortcomings. Today the Tiki, considered kitsch ten years ago, has made a big comeback and the recipes have undeniably become more subtle. It's time to depart for the South Seas and why not celebrate the voyage with the Fog Cutter, created by friend Vic during World War II? If you get lost along the way in the fog, I won't be responsible for any complaints (and neither will my publisher). The sherry should be poured over the cocktail in the glass, before adding the garnish.

## PREPARATION

Shake in a cocktail shaker (except the sherry), serve with the ice cubes from the shaker in a Tiki or Collins glass

## PRESENTATION

Garnish with a sprig of mint and add a straw (optional)

## DIFFICULTY

Difficult

## STYLE

Tropical delirium

## TASTE

Citrus and almonds mask the alcoholic strength

FINISH

Spicy yet fresh, quite controlled despite the amount of alcohol

# 38

# French 75

## INGREDIENTS

60ml (2 fl oz) gin, 15ml
(½ fl oz) lemon juice,
1 teaspoon sugar syrup,
150ml (5 fl oz) brut
Champagne

The first 'Champagne Cocktail' could not have been simpler: an Angostura-soaked sugar cube placed in the bottom of a Champagne flute or coupe that was then filled with Champagne. Try it, it's easy to make and rather good. The number of formulas has increased ever since, whether it's simply a question of brightening up the Champagne with a few drops of something else or of adding a touch of sparkle to the cocktail. The Champagne cocktail is more or less Champagne, more or less cocktail, depending....

Whatever the case, the French 75 remains one of the most popular and most effective recipes in the second category, despite arguments about its origins as well as the way of serving it. The French, English and Americans all dispute its invention. The first recipe published as a French 75 comes from an American book dating from 1927 (at the height of Prohibition), although a plain '75', created in Paris, had been mixed since 1922, involving a rather strange mixture of gin, calvados, absinthe and grenadine. A pretty explosive combo. And the consensus is, quite rightly, that different as they are, both drinks owe their name not to the number of the French *département* (Paris is 75) but to a 75mm French cannon used in the Great War.

For the French 75, there's no more debate about the base spirit: it is gin, the cognac was slipped into the recipe much later. The only issue still remaining concerns the serving glass: nowadays, as a matter of elegance, we are often treated to the flute. However, the cocktail was originally served in a tall glass filled with ice cubes (and yes, I can hear the shrieks of purists who are already struggling to accept that Champagne should be served as a cocktail). But let us not forget that the cocktail has never been an art for purists. That's just the way it is.

PREPARATION

**Shake in a cocktail shaker (except the Champagne), serve in a Collins glass filled with ice cubes and pour the Champagne over**

DIFFICULTY

**Moderate**

STYLE

**Explosive Champagne**

TASTE

**The Champagne's acidity tamed by the gin and sugar**

FINISH

**Dry, on notes of citrus**

# 39

# General Harrison's Egg Nogg

## INGREDIENTS

1 egg, 20ml (¾fl oz) sugar syrup, 120ml (4fl oz) cider, grated nutmeg to serve

It was about time for a recipe boasting a whole raw egg. First, a bit of genealogy: in the 17th century there was the Flip, a mixture of beer, rum, sugar and egg into which a red-hot poker was plunged to heat it up (subsequently – and this is difficult to believe, but easier to swallow – the Flip became considerably more elegant, to the extent of being transformed into a drink for 'delicate persons'). Somewhat earlier in the century, Shakespeare had his Lady Macbeth prepare poisoned possets. An eggy drink was a good way to hydrate and to ingest proteins ....

In the 19th century *lait de poule* was popular in France, while in the US it was known as Egg Nogg and in the Southern states became the indispensable Christmas drink. It was popular elsewhere – leaving a distinct impression on many a European traveller.

The gentry made their Egg Nogg with sugar, milk, an egg yolk and sherry or brandy (the use of whiskey was undeniable proof that one was in the presence of a redneck). It became the convention to grate a little fresh nutmeg over it (never, ever from a jar of supermarket spice that had been languishing in a cupboard for five years). It is utterly delicious and above all will keep you warm on a cold night.

The version here comes from the first book of cocktail recipes, published by Jerry Thomas in 1862. It is named in honour of an 1840 presidential candidate who presented himself as a simple 'man of the people' who liked to spend time on his porch drinking hard cider. This recipe would have allowed Harrison to drink it even in winter, although hardly on his porch since he came from Ohio, where it gets cold. He was elected president in 1841 but died one month after his inauguration. Not enough cider in Washington. (Take care: shaking something gassy can lead to a nasty surprise.)

**PREPARATION**

Shake in a cocktail shaker, serve in an Old Fashioned glass

**PRESENTATION**

Garnish with freshly grated nutmeg

**DIFFICULTY**

Difficult

**STYLE**

Liquid proteins for Christmas

**TASTE**

Very silky, slightly tingly, a touch of orchard flavour

**FINISH**

Cider and apple dominate, lots of pudding notes

# Gimlet

INGREDIENTS
......................................

60ml (2fl oz) gin, 15ml
(½fl oz) Rose's Lime
Cordial, lime slice
to serve

In 1867, one Lauchlan Rose patented the first method of preserving citrus juice without alcohol. His flagship product was a lime cordial known as Rose's Lime Cordial. Contrary to belief, his aim appears not to have been to counteract scurvy on board His Majesty's ships (Rose already provided the Admiralty with lemon juice preserved with rum), but to reach the wider Victorian health and anti-alcohol market – an irony in itself. An encounter between cordial and gin was inevitable, but its timing was uncertain. I imagine it was not long in coming, since in the UK someone is almost always suggesting that 'it would taste better with a drop of gin'. And they may well be right.

Unsurprisingly, it's the sailors who often get the blame; they were particularly partial to the concoction; the first recipe for which was published, belatedly in my opinion, in 1922. You will also note, as pointed out by several commentators, that there was a Navy doctor by the name of Thomas Gimlette. Don't expect me to establish a link from this; while the story is big on charm, it's low on facts. During the 1950s, as fans of *Mad Men* know, the Gimlet was a cocktail for women rather than tattooed mariners.

Over time, Mr Rose's cordial has fallen out of favour and nowadays bartenders tend to use fresh lime juice and sugar. Perhaps the legendary German bartender Charles Schumann found the perfect balance by mixing cordial and a little juice. As for me, I follow the prescription (but not the proportions) laid down by Raymond Chandler in *The Long Goodbye*: 'a real gimlet is half gin and half Rose's lime juice and nothing else'. Like his colleague William Faulkner, Chandler knew a fair bit about gin, although most of his characters seem to drink their alcohol straight.

PREPARATION

**Stir in a mixing glass**

TYPE OF GLASS

**Serve in a Martini or cocktail glass**

PRESENTATION

**Garnish with a slice of lime**

DIFFICULTY

**Moderate**

STYLE

**Guilty pleasure**

TASTE

**Dry and sweet at the same time, with notes of lime candy**

**FINISH**

**Long on the sugar and gin, brief on the citrus**

# 41

# Gin & Tonic

INGREDIENTS
.....................................

50ml (1¾fl oz) Citadelle
gin, 200ml tonic (7fl oz),
lime wedge and twist
to serve

Legend has it that to combat malaria, which was rife in India, British doctors mixed powdered cinchona bark with a little lime and water. Naturally, gin was added.... During the second half of the 19th century this quinine extract was used to flavour soda water, the fizzy drink popularized almost a century earlier and considered particularly good for the health. The modern Gin & Tonic was born. But now let's leave England and venture further afield ....

These days the G&T is a Spanish drink. Around 2005, the bartenders at a San Sebastian cocktail bar, aptly named Dickens, were intent upon putting some class back into a badly made drink and started using stemmed glasses. This trend rapidly shifted into high gear at Barcelona's Xix Bar, where splendidly large wine glasses are used to serve magnificent Gin & Tonics. And the practice spread all over the country. It was the beginning of a craze – and an attractive and elegant one, to boot. The size of the glass allows you to pour a proper measure of gin relative to the amount of tonic and the customer gets value for money.

Principles to respect when preparing at home: the glass should be large and filled with ice cubes; never in any circumstances use less than 50ml (1¾fl oz) good-quality gin (nowadays there are so many to choose from, from the 'driest' to more floral varieties) to 200ml (7fl oz) tonic; choose a premium tonic (Fever Tree, for example) that should be poured gently over the ice; use lemon or lime peel to garnish, instead of a quarter of lemon or lime. You can, if you wish, add the seed or grain of some spice (cardamom, pink pepper, juniper berry, etc.), more for its visual rather than aromatic appeal. It's best to stick to a classic line to avoid the fruit-salad effect.

**PREPARATION**

**Mix directly in a wine glass, serve over ice cubes**

**PRESENTATION**

**Garnish with a twist and wedge of lime**

**DIFFICULTY**

**Easy**

**STYLE**

**Long drink par excellence**

**TASTE**

**Dry, strong lemony and juniper notes**

**FINISH**

**Bitterness predominates (quinine). Relatively long**

# 42

# Gin Basil Smash

60ml (2fl oz) gin, 30ml
(1fl oz) lemon juice, 20ml
(¾fl oz) sugar syrup,
handful of basil leaves
plus sprig of basil
to serve

Classics evolve over a period of time but that doesn't stop certain recipes achieving a vertiginous ascent into the privileged category of modern classics. Such is the case of the Gin Basil Smash, created in 2008 and now enjoyed all over the world. If, as for bestsellers, no secret formula exists for a classic, there is one rule: simplicity. Simplicity in method, formula and ingredients – otherwise, how could your cocktail be made across the globe?

Jörg Meyer, creator of this recipe, owner of Hamburg's Le Lion bar and an outstanding figure on the German scene, has respected these principles while modernizing an old drinks family that was born in the 1840s but has been almost forgotten today. Historically, the Smash was ... a small Julep. Spirits, sugar and mint, with seasonal fruits to garnish. Perfectly refreshing. Faithful to the spirit of the Smash, as well as to the meaning of the word, Meyer lightly muddles in his shaker a half-lemon, a handful of red basil leaves and sugar syrup. He then adds gin, shakes vigorously and serves over fresh ice in an Old Fashioned glass.

Scarily simple, the Gin Basil Smash is a magical cocktail; delicious, refreshing, subtle. To try it is to adopt it. For an amateur to achieve the best result, I advise juicing the lemon first in order to control the balance, not forgetting to add the empty shell to the shaker and muddling it lightly with the basil, which need not be red. This allows you to gently extract the lemon's essential oils and to awaken the basil. As for the gin, a traditional brand will work perfectly well but a more herbaceous gin, such as Hendricks, gives a superb result. Don't hesitate to celebrate this ode to the return of fresh herbs in our cocktails.

**PREPARATION**

**Shake in a cocktail shaker (see left)**

**TYPE OF GLASS**

**Serve in an Old Fashioned glass filled with ice cubes**

**PRESENTATION**

**Garnish with a sprig of basil**

**DIFFICULTY**

**Difficult**

**STYLE**

**Refreshing cocktail**

**TASTE**

**Intense, lightly acidic but above all herby and fresh**

**FINISH**

Medium, citrus and basil

# 43

## Golden Cadillac

### INGREDIENTS

30ml (1fl oz) Galliano,
20ml (¾fl oz) Crème
de cacao, 30ml (1fl oz)
coconut milk, 30ml
(1fl oz) almond milk,
2 dashes orange bitters,
1 physalis to serve

Although it was invented in Tuscany at the very end of the 19th century, Galliano liqueur is closely linked to a totally 1970s concept of the (un)subtlety of the cocktail. There are plenty of 'classics' where it plays a central role: Harvey Wallbanger, Golden Dream and Golden Cadillac – all cocktails of little depth that flatter the palates of consumers in search of vodka's absence of taste or of an additional sugary kick in a world where sugar is already not lacking.

But Galliano, with its vanilla and aniseed notes, isn't bad in the hands of more elegant bartenders such as Ago Perrone, one of the best mixologists in London, who is also an ambassador for the brand. The company's other products, notably the coffee-flavoured Ristretto and the Balsamico (with balsamic vinegar) are definitely also worth a detour.

To return to our Golden Cadillac, so symbolic of the disco decade was it that it gave its name to a New York bar, which for several months tried to save the reputation of drinks that had gone out of fashion in discerning bars. That said, it was created around 1952, which makes it almost a pioneer among drinks. It was in a Californian restaurant; a newly married couple wanted the bartender to create a cocktail in their honour. It was named after the make and colour of their car (by now your imagination will be working overtime). As for the Golden Cadillac bar, we realized that things really had changed: the bar didn't last long. But the bartenders who worked there were no slouches (*see* the Harvey Wallbanger, page 102) and their version of this cocktail is less heavy and more interesting than the original, made with cream, which is replaced here with a mixture of coconut milk and almond milk. For a touch of complexity, add a couple of dashes of orange bitters.

PREPARATION

**Shake in a cocktail shaker**

TYPE OF GLASS

**Serve in a cocktail glass**

PRESENTATION

**Garnish with a physalis**

DIFFICULTY

**Moderate**

STYLE

**Kitsch cocktail**

TASTE

**Creamy but light, aniseed and lightly lemony**

FINISH

First almond, followed by cocoa, persistent

# 44

# The Good Life

**INGREDIENTS**

50ml (1¾fl oz) aquavit,
30ml (1fl oz) Domaine de
Canton ginger liqueur,
20ml (¾fl oz) lime juice,
15ml (½fl oz) sugar
syrup, 6 drops orange
bitters, orange peel
to serve

Calling a cocktail 'the good life' is taking a bit of a risk. On a sunny holiday, accompanied by the person you love, with 'your song' playing in the background and a light breeze blowing through the open windows, making the curtains ripple, the cocktail really has to rise to the occasion. The Good Life delivers the goods, even if it's not the best cocktail in this book. After all, the good life is not simply a collection of all the best things in life but a combination of various elements that combine to make you feel good. A bit like a good cocktail, somehow. The good life and the good cocktail both work the same way.

Chicago's Benjamin Schiller created this recipe. It includes an ingredient that very few people apart from Norwegians or Swedes would think of drinking when life is good. And yet it works. I'm talking about aquavit, which is essentially the Scandinavian gin, except that it is not flavoured with juniper berries but with caraway and/or dill. It is sometimes aged in cask, although for this recipe we must specify a clear aquavit such as the Danish Aalborg. In Scandinavia it is drunk neat with or after a typical meal.

In this recipe the aquavit is tamed by a good dose of Domaine de Canton, a superb ginger liqueur produced in France, although it is American (it was launched by John Cooper, brother of Ron Cooper of Saint Germain fame, his great rival and best enemy). A little sugar and lime juice to balance it, a few drops of orange bitters for the depth and complexity, and that's it. Ah, life is good sometimes, it's true.

**PREPARATION**

Shake in a cocktail shaker

**TYPE OF GLASS**

Serve in a cocktail glass

**PRESENTATION**

Garnish with a twist of orange peel

**DIFFICULTY**

Difficult

**STYLE**

Refreshing, spicy cocktail

**TASTE**

Jammy ginger and citrus, gourmand

**FINISH**

Medium, still ginger, cumin and slight persistent sharpness

# 45

# Green Beast

20ml (¾ fl oz) Pernod
absinthe, 20ml (¾ fl oz)
sugar syrup, 20ml
(¾ fl oz) lime juice, 80ml
(2½ fl oz) fresh water,
cucumber slices to serve

No spirit has been more abused by history, politics and propaganda than absinthe. There's not enough room here to correct all the errors and legends that are still being peddled about it today, but here are a few key points: absinthe does not send you mad; 19th-century absinthes have been tested and found to contain no more thujone, a harmful substance, than is legally permitted today; the majority of problems recorded were due to alcohol abuse and the poor quality of counterfeit spirits; the crusade against absinthe was largely led by a wine lobby in desperate straits after the phylloxera crisis.

A well-made absinthe is an absolutely delicious spirit. If drunk according to the rules, with four parts water and – why not? – a little sugar, it will be no stronger than a glass of wine. The essential thing is not to abuse it (and this goes for all alcohol) but to appreciate the producer's expertise and therefore not to engage in stupid practices such as flaming it, which serve only to hide the defects of bad versions. Good absinthes are becoming increasingly numerous but are rather expensive because of taxes and the use of quality ingredients. However, as it is used sparingly in classic cocktails, where it is often an important ingredient, a bottle can last a long time. Unless, like me, you become hooked on a cocktail that manages to make absinthe sexy again, now that France has finally authorized producers to use that name once more. With the Green Beast, Charles Vexenat found an unbeatable combination. A punch for sharing, it can also be made in individual servings.

An aniseed cocktail, but not overly so, extremely refreshing and perfectly balanced: it is not surprising that Pernod used it to promote its new absinthe.

**PREPARATION**

**Stir directly in a wine glass or a Collins glass**

**PRESENTATION**

**Serve over ice, garnish with thin slices of cucumber**

**DIFFICULTY**

**Moderate**

**STYLE**

**'Green fairy' punch**

**TASTE**

**Perfectly balanced, herbs and liquorice**

**FINISH**

**Intense and aniseed-flavoured but almost light**

# 46

# Hanky Panky

INGREDIENTS
..................................................

60ml (2fl oz) G'Vine
Nouaison gin, 30ml
(1fl oz) red vermouth,
2 drops Fernet Branca,
maraschino cherry to
serve (optional)

Before World War I American bars were not noted for tolerating difference. The races did not mix (although a white man could of course be served by a black one), nor did the different social classes; women were not welcome, as customers or employees. The bar was a masculine world and those of the fair sex to be found there could only be members of one profession, that of the prostitute. It took Prohibition to change things, one of its few positive effects.

In English pubs it was a different story: comely young ladies served the patrons at the bar. Yankee tourists making their first visit to the Savoy Hotel's American Bar got the shock of their life: the head barman was a bar mistress. Ada Coleman remained at her post from 1903 to 1926, to the great satisfaction of her English customers. Sadly, she finally had to make way for Harry Craddock, the star bartender who left the US following Prohibition and who, despite his English origins, did not look kindly on a feminine presence behind the bar. Had he forgotten the egalitarian world of the pubs?

Ada created the Hanky Panky, her most famous cocktail, for the actor-manager Sir Charles Hawtrey, Noel Coward's mentor. It's a twist on the Sweet Martini, balanced by the addition of the more bitter Fernet Branca. Hawtrey, who was looking for something 'with a bit of a punch', certainly got his money's worth. The Hanky Panky is back in fashion and many bartenders have even aged it in barrels, sometimes with very good results. That said, there's no need to go quite that far to appreciate it.

**PREPARATION**

**Stir in a mixing glass**

**TYPE OF GLASS**

**Serve in a wine or cocktail glass**

**PRESENTATION**

**Garnish with a maraschino cherry (optional)**

**DIFFICULTY**

**Moderate**

**STYLE**

**Sweet, strong aperitif**

**TASTE**

**Dry at first, then sweeter, juniper, pine and orange notes**

**FINISH**

**Intensely herby without being too bitter**

# 47 Harvey Wallbanger

## INGREDIENTS

60ml (2fl oz) filtered
orange juice (see right),
1 teaspoon lemon juice,
45ml (1½fl oz) vodka,
15ml (½fl oz) Galliano,
1 dash orange bitters,
orange slice and salt
to serve (optional)

In theory, twisting a cocktail should be a simple business: replace or add an ingredient and pray that it works. The Screwdriver barely deserves the title of cocktail. After all, it's simply a vodka orange (in other words, orange juice spiced up with ethanol). Add a little Galliano, a liqueur tasting of vanilla and aniseed, and you've got a Harvey Wallbanger, the great classic of the Italian brand and emblem of the 1970s cocktail years.

Like the Golden Cadillac (*see* page 94), the story goes that it was invented in California in 1952. The painstaking work of Robert Simonson, cocktail correspondent of the *New York Times* (a job to die for), gives us to believe that the cocktail was born in the marketing department of the American importer of Galliano, towards the end of the 1960s. A triumph: for more than fifteen years the Harvey Wallbanger was everywhere. One can only hope that the 'marketeer' got a good promotion. It had, of course, a place of honour on the menu of the Golden Cadillac.

How do you make something interesting out of what is essentially no more than a mixture of flavourless alcohol, orange juice (known for its lack of intensity in a cocktail) and a little liqueur? Don Lee, mad scientist and renowned bartender, clarifies the orange juice in a centrifuge or with agar-agar. This not only alters the texture and the intensity of the taste, which gives the cocktail a lift, but also produces a perfectly clear juice that can be stirred rather than shaken to make a far more elegant drink. Although you can find methods online, the techniques may be too complex for beginners, so the recipe I suggest here is the homemade alternative offered by Lee, which consists of straining the orange juice through a coffee filter before mixing it with lemon juice. Science meets DIY!

**PREPARATION**

**Shake in a cocktail shaker**

**TYPE OF GLASS**

**Serve in a Collins or cocktail glass**

**PRESENTATION**

**Garnish with a slice of orange lightly sprinkled with coarse salt (optional)**

**DIFFICULTY**

**Difficult**

**STYLE**

**Kitsch cocktail**

**TASTE**

**Basically citrussy, some background spice notes**

**FINISH**

Short, a touch of vanilla above the orange

# 48 Hemingway Special

INGREDIENTS

60ml (2fl oz) Havana
Club 3 Años, 30ml
(1fl oz) lime juice, 15ml
(½fl oz) maraschino
liqueur, 15ml (½fl oz)
grapefruit juice, lime
peel or 1 maraschino
cherry to serve

Hemingway's name certainly crops up frequently in this little book. We've already said that the Daiquiri is the base formula for many cocktails. The long-awaited encounter between the writer and this cocktail took place in Havana's El Floridita in 1932. Constante Ribalaigua, who reigned supreme as owner, offered four different, numbered Daiquiris. The #1 was the classic while the #4 was made in a blender, with a little maraschino liqueur. The #2 added a little orange juice to the basic recipe, while grapefruit juice was used in the #3, originally dedicated to the musician Benjamin Orbon.

The story goes that one day Hemingway was made a #3 by Antonio Meilan, the nephew of Constante's wife. Hemingway, nicknamed 'Papa' in Cuba, enjoyed it but, being diabetic, found it too sugary. He declared that the cocktail would be better with twice as much rum and no sugar. And so the Papa Doble was born. Hemingway, of course, was pretty particular and had an alcohol problem that cannot be described as slight. The bar's impeccable reputation was therefore at risk: word of the new cocktail was bound to spread fast and they would have to serve thirsty tourists with gigantic double doses of rum. What to do?

The fact that the Papa Doble never appeared on the bar's menu showed good sense: it limited the risks associated with making such a strong drink available to customers and allowed bartenders to 'lie' when someone insisted on being served the drink invented for Hemingway – they could make up something else. Is this speculation? Who knows? At all events, after Papa won the Nobel Prize in 1954, a Hemingway Special was to be found on the menu, that is, a Daiquiri #3 with normal proportions but without sugar.

**PREPARATION**

Shake in a cocktail shaker with crushed ice

**TYPE OF GLASS**

Serve in a cocktail glass

**PRESENTATION**

Garnish with a twist of lime peel or a maraschino cherry

**DIFFICULTY**

Moderate

**STYLE**

Refreshment for aspiring writers

**TASTE**

Tart and dry but balanced

**FINISH**

The herbaceous notes of the maraschino dominate, contrasted with the lime and grapefruit

# 49 Irish Mermaid

## INGREDIENTS

30ml (1fl oz) Irish
whiskey, 2 teaspoons
Cherry Heering,
2 teaspoons Aperol,
1 teaspoon orgeat
(almond syrup),
2 dashes Angostura
bitters, orange peel and
maraschino cherries
to serve

In the beginning, there was no such thing as the modern cocktail shaker. The first bartenders to serve mixed drinks prepared with ice cubes used glasses of different sizes to create a sort of primitive version. But to be more spectacular (not necessarily more effective), someone invented the technique of the roll or 'throwing', consisting of taking a glass in each hand and pouring liquid from one to the other with a long vertical action to impress the customer.

The advent of shakers killed off this technique, except in Cuba where it became a trick of the local *cantineros*. They certainly didn't inherit it from their American colleagues, but many immigrant Asturians used a similar technique to serve their (not very fizzy) cider. Being 'thrown' from a height of five feet aerated the liquid, opened it out and made it more pleasant to drink. But even in Cuba the roll disappeared, especially when the blender became popular. Only the Boadas bar in Barcelona, founded by an old El Floridita hand, kept it alive for more than fifty years. And it's from there that the technique once again set out to conquer the world.

Today it is fashionable pretty much everywhere although often badly executed (bartenders who spill a good bit of your cocktail over their feet or who fail to chill the drink properly because they're too busy). Max La Rocca is an Italian bartender but he has worked in Barcelona for a long time and uses the roll to prepare his Irish Mermaid. When he makes it like this the cocktail is perfectly chilled but less diluted than if it had been shaken. It also acquires an appetising foam top. Max is an expert. Try it, but at your own risk. If you are sensible, you'll stick with the mixing glass. Whatever method you use, the Irish Mermaid is an excellent cocktail that Max has managed to introduce to many bars.

PREPARATION

**Stir in a mixing glass**

TYPE OF GLASS

**Serve in a cocktail glass**

PRESENTATION

**Garnish with maraschino cherries and a squeeze of orange peel over the surface of the cocktail**

DIFFICULTY

**Moderate**

STYLE

**Rich, luscious cocktail**

TASTE

**Sweet and polished, majoring on red fruits and dried fruits**

**FINISH**

**Relatively long, malty, with good almond persistence**

**INGREDIENTS**

60ml (2fl oz) cognac,
15ml (½fl oz) orgeat
(almond) syrup, 2 dashes
Angostura bitters,
lemon peel to serve

Cocktails created to commemorate a special event are always in fashion and sometimes the results are good. More rarely, they survive long term. For example, the Japanese, which was created on the occasion of the first visit of an official Japanese delegation to the United States in 1860. According to David Wondrich, it was led by Tateishi Noriyuki, a great lover of women and cocktails. The young man, nicknamed Tommy, may have visited the bar of the illustrious Jerry Thomas, which was close to the delegation's hotel, and Jerry may (the tense is always conditional) have invented our cocktail.

Looking at the ingredients, one wonders what's Japanese about them. A supply of sake or umeshu (plum liqueur) was probably not available at the time. It's true that the colour of the mixture is yellowish, and sensitivity to this kind of insult was probably the last thing New York bartenders of the time would worry about. The name is not the only strange thing: cognac, orgeat, Angostura and nothing else. What a combination! To be honest, it is a lot more normal than you might think at first sight.

Remember the first definition of the cocktail: spirits, sugar, bitters and water. The Japanese offers the same combination, except that it replaces the sugar with orgeat syrup. Given the date of its creation, this is perhaps one of the first important twists to the cocktail's base formula. For some palates it will lack sharpness and in a good number of bars several drops of lemon juice are added. The result is, obviously, very good but it takes us a bridge too far: it's no longer a twist, but a change of concept. Well-diluted (so shake vigorously), the Japanese needs nothing else. The freshness of lemon will come from the essential oils of the twist placed on the surface of this splendid cognac/almond mix.

PREPARATION

**Shake in a cocktail shaker**

TYPE OF GLASS

**Serve in a cocktail glass**

PRESENTATION

**Garnish with a twist of lemon peel**

DIFFICULTY

**Moderate**

STYLE

**Rich cocktail**

TASTE

**Ample, candied fruits and marzipan**

FINISH

**Average length, on the spices (vanilla, clove), slight bitterness**

# 51 Le Jardin de Mémé

**INGREDIENTS**

40ml (1¼fl oz) green Chartreuse, 15ml (½fl oz) St Germain elderflower liqueur, 30ml (1fl oz) lime juice, 1 teaspoon sugar syrup, 2 dashes absinthe, 3 basil leaves plus extra to serve, egg white

For several years a French bar called Candelaria seems to have held squatter's rights over the rest of the world's best drinking establishments. And I must admit that Candelaria is, and has been since opening in 2011, one of the best bars I know. The team changes but the quality stays the same, undoubtedly due to the shrewdness of the partners, Carina Soto Velasquez, Josh Fontaine and Adam Tsou.

Carina and Josh cut their teeth in the Expérimental group (*see* St-Germain-des-Prés, page 174) and wanted to open something less classic yet distinctive. Candelaria is a tiny but excellent taqueria (a taco restaurant) whose back door leads to a splendid cocktail bar. Although little known in Paris, the concept of the hidden bar is not original (*see* Paddington, page 142). Despite what a cocktail snob might consider a handicap, the team has given the place its own personality, especially by bidding farewell to the stuffy side of American speakeasies and emphasizing its party spirit.

The cocktails are big on herbs and homemade syrups, with a logical (I hear you say) predilection for Mexican-influenced ingredients. However, I have not gone for one of their excellent mescal-based cocktails but instead opted for one of Josh Fontaine's iconic recipes, Le Jardin de Mémé (Grandma's Garden). The name suits the ingredients well. This cocktail is modern and refreshing, yet not at all aggressive, in spite of the Chartreuse liqueur's 55 per cent ABV. The Candelaria team also owns two more Parisian bars: the Glass in Pigalle (hot dog, beer, cocktails and party central), and the Mary Celeste, whose slogan 'eat and drink well in the Marais' simply says it all.

PREPARATION

**Shake in a cocktail shaker**

TYPE OF GLASS

**Serve in a cocktail glass**

PRESENTATION

**Garnish with a basil leaf**

DIFFICULTY

**Difficult**

STYLE

**Herby, floral cocktail**

TASTE

**Relatively silky and round, intensely herbaceous, with a touch of aniseed**

FINISH

**Slight acidity, herbaceous, floral, then gourmand**

# 52 Knickerbocker

INGREDIENTS

60ml (2fl oz) Jamaican
rum, 30ml (1fl oz) lime
juice, 15ml (½fl oz)
curaçao, 15ml (½fl oz)
raspberry syrup, lime
peel or seasonal fruits
to serve

First things first: what is a Knickerbocker? In 1809 Washington Irving published a satirical history of New York under the pseudonym Diedrich Knickerbocker. The surname became synonymous with a certain type of snobbish New Yorker – aristocratic, often of Dutch origin and, of course, comfortably off. Despite the pejorative connotation, the target market happily adopted the nickname and many clubs or drinking dens were opened featuring the word prominently in their names.

Of course (we are in the US), one day, probably in the 1850s, someone invented a drink they called the Knickerbocker. I came across it for the first time in an excellent book on lost cocktails written by Ted Haigh. I was very surprised: it was a Tiki cocktail nearly ninety years before the invention of the concept. If you want proof, look at the Mai Tai and compare the recipes. The Dutch in New York inspired a tropical cocktail. Sometimes one wonders what goes on in bartenders' heads.

The Knickerbocker betrays its age by the presence of raspberry syrup, one of the favourite weapons of the first mixologists: it was the grenadine of its day. Its alcoholic ingredient also betrays the social class of the public it was aimed at: on the East coast rum was for the gentry, the more ... problematic classes drank whiskey. We also imagine that in 1850 lime juice was not exactly cheap. Social history is interesting but it isn't everything. You will see – and this is really the point – that a well-proportioned Knickerbocker, a trailblazer in its day, has become a true classic to which we love to return.

**PREPARATION**

Shake in a cocktail shaker

**TYPE OF GLASS**

Serve in a cocktail glass, filled with crushed ice if liked

**PRESENTATION**

Garnish with fruits in season or a twist of lime peel

**DIFFICULTY**

Moderate

**STYLE**

Tropical before its time

**TASTE**

Refreshing acidity, fruity

**FINISH**

Medium, the very rich rum gleaming in the background

# 53 Last Word

INGREDIENTS

**30ml (1fl oz) Aviation gin, 30ml (1fl oz) green Chartreuse, 30ml (1fl oz) maraschino liqueur, 30ml (1fl oz) lime juice, lime peel to serve**

At the foot of the Grand Som, a mountain in the Chartreuse, the silent monks of the Carthusian order have been busy for nearly three centuries producing Chartreuse, one of the world's most famous herbal liqueurs. It would be hard to imagine the monks giving a helping hand to Al Capone, yet the link between the Carthusians and American Prohibition is not as far-fetched as it seems.

During those years the bar of the Detroit Athletic Club is reputed to have continued, like many others, to serve alcohol and cocktails. One drink made it famous: the Last Word, a mixture of equal parts of gin, maraschino liqueur, lime juice and green Chartreuse. Vaudeville artist Frank Fogarty is said to have discovered the drink at the club before enthusiastically introducing it to the speakeasies of New York. This story, cloaked in alcoholic fumes, is doubtful and the truth remains elusive, but the first official appearance of the recipe dates from 1951, in Ted Saucier's *Bottoms Up*, a book decorated with stunning pin-ups. Sadly, the cocktail was forgotten almost as soon as it was published. The Last Word disappeared from circulation for fifty years, until Seattle bartender Murray Stenson saved it in 2004.

And voilà! The Last Word conquered the US before reaching Europe. It's been reinterpreted since and has become a classic, even a symbol of the cocktail renaissance, since it uses historic liqueurs snubbed by the bartenders of the wilderness years of the last four decades of the 20th century. And it is a minor miracle. Today, while the monks maintain their silence, the laity whisper that the Last Word is the world's most popular Chartreuse cocktail. From there, it's just a small step to building a state-of-the-art new monastery wing for soon to be wordless novices. And that is the last word on the matter.

PREPARATION

**Shake in a cocktail shaker**

TYPE OF GLASS

**Serve in a cocktail glass**

PRESENTATION

**Garnish with a twist of lime peel**

DIFFICULTY

**Moderate**

STYLE

**Complex herbal cocktail**

TASTE

**Powerful, on the herbs and gin**

FINISH

Long and dry, the maraschino herbs take control

# 54 Louis Special

## INGREDIENTS

30ml (1fl oz) Aviation
gin, 30ml (1fl oz) red
vermouth, 30ml (1fl oz)
orange juice, 3 dashes
curaçao, 3 dashes
Crème de noyau,
3 dashes Angostura
bitters, lemon slice and
1 maraschino cherry
to serve

In the days when the Champs-Élysées had yet to acquire its glamorous reputation, there stood, some 500 metres (¹/₃ mile) from the Place de l'Étoile, a coachmen's tavern. In 1899 it was bought by Louis Fouquet, owner of the Criterion in Rue Saint Lazare, who transformed it into an American-style bar and grill. Fouquet's Criterion became the go-to meeting place for everyone in the small world that revolved around horses and racing. Historically, jockeys, racehorse-owners and fanatical racegoers were among the first Europeans to take an interest in mixed drinks. It was the same in the United States, although they did not dominate the landscape of the enlightened drinker quite so much. Happily for his new clientele, Fouquet was one of the leading bartenders of Paris.

In 1896 Fouquet published *Bariana*, the second book of cocktail recipes published in France, though undoubtedly the first in terms of influence. Sadly, he died of typhoid fever in 1905 and his wife quickly followed him to the grave. As perceptive readers will have guessed, his establishment survived him, although it is no longer a place where the great formulas of its founder are honoured. Fouquet and his contemporaries modelled their art on American recipes brought to Europe during World Fairs.

However, Fouquet never failed to add a French flourish, especially the Crème de noyau, a liqueur now rarely encountered but still produced under the Noyau de Poissy label, in what was until recently the only craft distillery in Île-de-France. Louis used it in his signature cocktail to flavour a delicious mixture of gin, vermouth and orange juice, which prefigures the much more famous – and less good – Bronx. Raise a glass in memory of this pioneer whose work does not get the attention in bars that it deserves.

PREPARATION

**Stir in a mixing glass**

TYPE OF GLASS

**Serve in a cocktail glass**

PRESENTATION

**Garnish with a slice of lemon and a maraschino cherry**

DIFFICULTY

**Moderate**

STYLE

**Classic French-style cocktail**

TASTE

**Bitter orange, with background spices**

**FINISH**

**Orange marmalade with floral notes**

# 55 La Louisiane

INGREDIENTS

30ml (1fl oz) rye
whiskey, 30ml (1fl oz)
Benedictine, 30ml
(1fl oz) red vermouth,
2 dashes absinthe,
2 dashes Peychaud's
bitters, maraschino
cherries to serve

New Orleans – what would we do without it? Or Louisiana. With its Spanish, French, Anglo-Saxon and even Italian and German influences, it gave birth to the distinctive Creole cocktail. This book features no fewer than five cocktails linked to its capital. All became classics thanks to their creators' skill at maintaining the balance between tradition and innovation (sometimes even with a nod to revolution: *see* Brandy Crusta, page 48).

The Louisiana cocktail is characterized by the use of specific ingredients. The base spirit was originally cognac, replaced by rye whiskey after the ravages of phylloxera in French vineyards. Absinthe was used as flavouring until it was banned (in 1912 in the US) and replaced by Herbsaint, a local substitute. The liqueurs are often equally French, Benedictine or Picon being particularly popular. As for the bitters, Peychaud's, a product invented around 1830 by a Creole pharmacist, took the place of Angostura (its profile is slightly aniseed and a little sweeter). Louisiana was also one of the first overseas markets for Italian or French vermouth.

All of which explains how La Louisiane is so typical of (yes, you guessed it) Louisiana. The recipe was published for the first time in 1937, but I would place a bet on it being much older. It bears all the hallmarks of the American cocktail at the end of the 19th century. It was the house cocktail of an eponymous French restaurant founded in New Orleans in 1881, and still open.

I discovered La Louisiane in 2010 at Becketts Kop, one of the best bars in Berlin, and I still haven't quite got over it. I'm not alone in this: it shows up more and more on the lists of cocktails 'to be saved', both in France and the US. Try it and you'll understand why.

PREPARATION

**Stir in a mixing glass**

TYPE OF GLASS

**Serve in a cocktail glass**

PRESENTATION

**Garnish with maraschino cherries**

DIFFICULTY

**Moderate**

STYLE

**Sweet, strong digestif**

TASTE

**Rounded, sugary, herby**

**FINISH**

**Complex, slight but persistent bitterness, aniseed notes**

# Mai Tai

INGREDIENTS
.................................

30ml (1fl oz) Jamaican rum, 30ml (1fl oz) aged agricultural rum, 30ml (1fl oz) lime juice, 15ml (½fl oz) orgeat (almond syrup), 15ml (½fl oz) curaçao, 1 teaspoon sugar syrup, ½ lime and mint sprig or a flower to serve

There was quite a bust-up around the Mai Tai, involving Don the Beachcomber and Trader Vic, the biggest promoters of the Tiki cocktail. But the drink we know today is the creation of Vic, who claimed that he invented it in 1944 for a couple of Tahitian friends. At the first sip, the woman exclaimed 'Maita'i roa ae!' ('excellent!'). Decide for yourself.

The Mai Tai is one of my favourite cocktails. It reveals the full potential of the tropical cocktail in terms of flavour and texture without a trace of excess (it's not too strong or too sweet, and it's not a hotch potch where too many ingredients jostle for position so you can't see the wood for the trees). It's a hymn to balance, clearly based on the structure of the Daiquiri: rum, sugar, lime. As we have already seen, Vic learned plenty at Havana's El Floridita bar. For the nutty notes that make a perfect accompaniment to the rum, he added orgeat. A touch of orange curaçao adds another almost caramelized citrus dimension.

Historically, Vic used a very complex Jamaican rum, Wray & Nephew's 17-year-old. Unfortunately this classic disappeared down the gullets of our grandparents. To recreate the experience, Tiki experts such as Jeff Berry recommend mixing agricultural and Jamaican rum. Vic would have made the same choice after exhausting his stock, although recent research indicates that he might have used a very rare Martinique rum, distilled from molasses. If this were true, the cocktail's profile would be very different. In any case, you are free to use the combination that suits you best, but the line recommended by Berry has proved itself. A word of advice, however: no Captain Morgan. You need character and quality. Treat the Mai Tai with respect and it will repay you a hundred-fold.

PREPARATION

**Shake in a cocktail shaker**

TYPE OF GLASS

**Serve in an Old Fashioned filled with ice cubes**

PRESENTATION

**Garnish with half a squeezed lime and a sprig of mint, or a flower**

DIFFICULTY

**Difficult**

STYLE

**King of the Tiki cocktails**

TASTE

**Ample, caramelized almond and orange, lightly smoked rum**

**FINISH**

**Bitter almonds, slight tanginess and complexity, due to the rums**

# 57 Manhattan

## INGREDIENTS

60ml (2fl oz) rye
whiskey, 30ml (1fl oz)
red vermouth, 2 dashes
Angostura bitters,
1 maraschino cherry or
orange peel to serve

If I had to choose just one cocktail, it would be the Manhattan. But it must be made with two parts rye whiskey, one part sweet vermouth and two good dashes of aromatic bitters. A Manhattan made with bourbon, as common as rye whiskey is rare and expensive, is perfectly honourable but not for me. It is too sweet, too vanilla, too round; rye's character and spiciness are essential. Before I tried it like this, I did not understand why this cocktail, alongside the Martini, was one of the two absolute classics made with vermouth. I have since seen the light.

The first Manhattan recipe was published in 1884, in O.H. Byron's *The Modern Bartenders' Guide*. Its exact origins are unknown – and don't trust the stories going round, they are all false. Obviously there was a Manhattan Club in New York, but the name is so common and such a no-brainer that the recipe could have come from any other bar of the time. What is certain is that whiskey and vermouth were bound to meet sometime. A fortified aromatic wine, both bitter and sweet, vermouth was the fashionable aperitif of the 1870s. Until then, what was called a cocktail consisted of a drink in which bitters, liqueurs and sugar lifted and spiced up, so to speak, the spirit. It was a question of rounding off the angles, of polishing up the base ingredient.

The introduction of vermouth raised the bar: a true symbiosis that gave a whole new result. To borrow a term from the world of whisky, the Manhattan and its contemporaries were the first cocktails to be blended. This discreet revolution helped to smash the dividing lines between the families of 'mixed drinks' and launched us along the road to modernity. That said, the survival of the Manhattan is not down to its historic value but to its timeless, eternal character.

PREPARATION

Stir in a mixing glass

TYPE OF GLASS

Serve in a cocktail or Martini glass

PRESENTATION

Garnish with a maraschino cherry or a strip of orange peel

DIFFICULTY

Moderate

STYLE

Strong, dry aperitif

TASTE

Powerful and spicy, with orange and vanilla notes

FINISH

Average length, with very spicy notes and a slight persistent tartness

# 58 Martinez

60ml (2fl oz) red
vermouth, 30ml (1fl oz)
Old Tom gin, 1 teaspoon
maraschino liqueur, 2
dashes Boker's bitters,
maraschino cherry or
lemon slice to serve

Just this once, we'll start with the recipe: in its base form, made with two parts sweet vermouth to one part gin, the Martinez is a cocktail with character that has the advantage of being relatively low in alcohol – taking dilution into account it works out at around 19 per cent ABV. By way of comparison, the Manhattan comes in at around 25 per cent ABV. The two cocktails appeared for the first time in 1884, in the same book, although the Manhattan went through some changes before stabilizing circa 1910. But to a moustachioed New Yorker of the 1890s, if he looked long enough the Martinez would still be by and large recognizable. And with reason: in evolving it changed its name and the Dry Martini is more than likely its grandson.

The story is simple. During the 1880s, the American palate preferred sweet things. The most popular style of gin was not the London Dry that everyone drinks today, but rather Old Tom, with a little added sugar to boot. The vermouth of the day was not French (therefore dry) but Italian. It is *de rigueur* to add liqueurs (maraschino or curaçao but also Crème de noyau in Europe), which are by definition sugary. The presence of bitters doesn't change much. And there you have the Martinez. In the following decade, dryness took over. Old Tom was replaced by London Dry gin, sweet vermouth by dry (often over one hundred grams less sugar per litre) and the liqueur disappeared. And there's the Martini! As we know, the drying process would continue until (sacrilege!) the vermouth almost disappeared.

Nowadays, with moustaches back in fashion, the Martinez is beginning to poke its nose out again, even if some people serve it with more gin than vermouth. Cry 'Shame on you!' and insist on the real thing. You'll thank me.

**PREPARATION**

Stir in a mixing glass

**TYPE OF GLASS**

Serve in a cocktail glass

**PRESENTATION**

Garnish with a maraschino cherry or a slice of lemon

**DIFFICULTY**

Moderate

**STYLE**

Sweet, complex aperitif

**TASTE**

Round and herbaceous, with juniper and orange notes

**FINISH**

Slightly sugary with a touch of residual bitterness

# 59 Mary Pickford

60ml (2fl oz) Havana
Club 3 Años, 30ml
(1fl oz) pineapple juice,
2 teaspoons maraschino
liqueur, 1 teaspoon
grenadine

'America's Sweetheart' was the greatest star of the silent screen. Her golden curls and angelic air hid a formidable character and great intelligence. Fortified by her early success she founded United Artists in 1919, together with Charlie Chaplin, Douglas Fairbanks and D.W. Griffith, the legendary and controversial director of *Birth of a Nation*. Her 1920 marriage to Fairbanks, the king of Hollywood, only increased her aura. They formed the most powerful couple in the business, their every move monitored by an army of fans. As movie royalty, they made regular long trips around the world.

They even went to the Soviet Union, where in 1926 they made a cameo appearance in *A Kiss from Mary Pickford*, a comedy by Sergei Komarov about a young actress who wants to follow in the star's footsteps. But it was probably during the winter of 1922–3 that the couple visited Cuba for a brief vacation. They each returned with a cocktail named in their honour (Douglas Fairbanks's is also included in this book, *see* page 74). Still popular today, the Mary Pickford cocktail is a superb example of the Cuban School – although created by a British bartender, it went straight into the local repertoire.

The light Cuban rum forms an ideal base to which pineapple juice is added, preferably fresh (this is a lot of work but it's worth the trouble; if you are in a hurry, make sure that the juice you buy contains no added sugar). To add sweetness, correct the acidity and also to give some herbaceous notes, the drink needs a good dollop of maraschino, one of the most common liqueurs in the Cuban cocktail repertoire. Finally, as in a number of other cocktails of the same origin, the grenadine lends a dash of colour. Choose a genuine pomegranate syrup rather than the red fruit syrups available in supermarkets.

*see* page 74

PREPARATION

**Shake in a cocktail shaker**

TYPE OF GLASS

**Serve in a cocktail glass**

DIFFICULTY

**Moderate**

STYLE

**Tropical cocktail**

TASTE

**Almost dirty yet creamy, with almond notes**

**FINISH**

**Long, herby with a touch of bitterness**

# 60 Mint Julep

INGREDIENTS

75ml (2½fl oz) bourbon,
15ml (½fl oz) sugar
syrup, 2 sprigs mint plus
extra to serve

In his seminal *The Gentleman's Companion* (1939), Charles H. Baker Jr., journalist, socialite and friend of Hemingway, described the Mint Julep as one of 'humanity's truly civilized inventions', adding that some people would be ready to shoot it out over ways to make it. In other words, to be civilized means being willing to die for your cocktail cause. Baker surely didn't mean to say that but it is certainly a question of identity: at the time, the Mint Julep had become a symbol of the peaceful and friendly culture of the American South, the positive side of the Civil War's aftermath. The loser's consolatory potion. Grass did not grow under the hooves of the northern generals, only mint! We see two Juleps in the first scene of *Gone with the Wind*, in order to leave no doubt about the region where the story will unfold. When John Ford made a slightly paternalistic film about a Southern judge, each unsettling comment is softened by the Julep held in the protagonist's hand.

But from Louisiana to Maryland, by way of Georgia and Kentucky, there seemed to be no agreement as to how a Julep was made: what kind of mint, spirits (bourbon, rye, cognac, gin, rum, peach brandy), type of glass, garnish .... The consensus is much greater today. Baker points out that the Julep is a concept that does not belong exclusively to the South and is still delicious even when prepared in a thousand different ways. And, even if it invaded the US via the South, Baker was somehow right: the Julep has been known for more than a thousand years. It was even mentioned in the works of Persian savant, Muhammad ibn Zakariya al-Razi.

Like the cocktail (which it precedes by centuries), the Julep's origins were medicinal. And that, in a nutshell, is the history of alcohol: a medicine that is so good that you still take it, even when not ill.

**PREPARATION**

Make directly in an Old Fashioned glass, lightly muddle the mint with the sugar, add the bourbon and crushed ice, mix together

**PRESENTATION**

Garnish with a sprig of mint and serve with a straw (optional)

**DIFFICULTY**

Difficult

**STYLE**

Refreshing on a hot and humid afternoon

**TASTE**

Bourbon softened by the sugar and mint

FINISH

Fresh and minty, with vanilla notes

# 61 Mojito

INGREDIENTS

40ml (1¼fl oz) Havana
Club 3 Años, 15ml
(½fl oz) lime juice,
2 teaspoons white sugar,
2 sprigs mint plus extra
to serve, 80ml (2½fl oz)
sparkling water, 1 dash
Angostura bitters

Everyone knows the Mojito, the most popular cocktail in the world. I want to tell you about the true Mojito, the Cuban Mojito. However, it is important to be clear: one doesn't drink better Mojitos in Cuba than elsewhere, even if all the backpackers (the careless ones) returning from this Caribbean paradise claim otherwise. Blame this on a planned economy that prefers to export the citrus crop rather than allow enough of it to the local bars, leaving them to use a kind of local lime squash.

The original concept of the Mojito must, however, be saved. The Mojito is an aperitif, to be drunk rapidly before food, which is why it is made in relatively small glasses, not with crushed ice but cubes broken up, if necessary, with the back of the mixing spoon. The sugar is always white. The drink is prepared with freshly squeezed juice and not with lime wedges which are then muddled with mint. And, correctly, the mint is very lightly pressed (rather than brutally crushed, which increases the bitterness). What's more, the Cubans, who use a particular variety of mint with rhubarb-coloured stalks, muddle the stalks rather than the leaf.

Preparation is as follows: place the mint, sugar, juice and a little sparkling water in the glass. Stir well with the spoon, lightly muddling the mint (leaves and stalks) until the sugar has been diluted. Next add the rum, then the ice cubes. Mix and top up with sparkling water. Garnish with a sprig of mint and a drop of Angostura. Drink quickly. For a slightly different but still Cuban Mojito, replace the lime with grapefruit. This is the so-called 'luxury' version served at the Concha beach club where the cocktail was supposed to have been invented (or, at any rate, popularized, but we're not going to reignite the debate).

**PREPARATION**

**Make directly in a Collins glass, serve over ice**

**PRESENTATION**

**Garnish with a sprig of mint**

**DIFFICULTY**

**Moderate**

**STYLE**

**Aperitif for a hot and humid climate**

**TASTE**

**Sparkling and minty, with slight acidity**

**FINISH**

The Cuban rum and mint dance the salsa

# Monkey's Gland

## INGREDIENTS

45ml (1½fl oz) gin, 45ml
(1½fl oz) orange juice,
1 teaspoon grenadine,
4 dashes absinthe,
maraschino cherry or
orange slice to serve

The popularity of the anti-ageing industry is nothing new. One of its pioneers was Serge Voronoff. He became famous at the beginning of the 20th century for his ideas on the therapeutic use of animal glands on humans to resolve hormonal and other problems – not only thyroid deficiencies but also ageing and therefore, of course, sexual vigour.

In June 1920, he transplanted slices of chimpanzee's testicles into the scrotum of a man. You can imagine how that captured the attention of the media – and of a number of elderly millionaires. After all, Viagra was not around at the time. Monkey glands became one of the cultural phenomena of the Roaring Twenties. They were of course dubbed roaring for a reason, if not several – jazz, alcohol, sex, drugs. Keith Richards invented nothing (except his music, of course).

It was therefore quite logical for a bartender to launch an eponymous cocktail, hitting upon a name that was certain to get people talking. It was Harry MacElhone and he was onto a winner; he had not yet bought the New York Bar in Rue Daunou, Paris, but was still working at Ciro's in London (where the upper crust danced, drank and frolicked together). The invigorating ingredient meant to represent the famous glands was none other than absinthe, banned in Paris since 1915 but still legal in the UK. In 1923, Harry moved to Paris, where the cocktail became popular. Other bartenders put it on their menus, including the highly respectable Frank Meier of the Ritz. Sadly, the law meant that the absinthe had to be replaced with aniseed aperitifs. It was a passion killer, in more ways than one. Today, you can again invoke the so-called green fairy if you are feeling the weight of the years, although I cannot guarantee the efficacy of the operation.

PREPARATION

**Shake in a cocktail shaker**

TYPE OF GLASS

**Serve in a cocktail or Martini glass**

PRESENTATION

**Garnish with a maraschino cherry or an orange slice**

DIFFICULTY

**Moderate**

STYLE

**Invigorating cocktail**

TASTE

**Aniseed and herbaceous, but lightened by the citrus**

FINISH

The gin manifests itself, followed by a touch of acidity and an aniseed note

# 63 Morning Glory Fizz

INGREDIENTS
.................................

60ml (2fl oz) blended
Scotch whisky, 15ml
(½fl oz) lemon juice,
2 teaspoons lime juice,
15ml (½fl oz) sugar
syrup, 3 dashes absinthe,
egg white, soda water,
orange or lemon peel
to serve

Here's a funny thing: as well as being a flower that opens in the early part of the day, morning glory is also a slang expression for the phenomenon of matutinal tumescence. In the context of drinks, a Morning Glory is a remedy for the excesses of the night before. Undoubtedly there's a certain logic here, but one that may not become apparent until circumstances are such that a tipple of this nature is called for. In any case, our recipe contains absinthe, a fact that will not be lost on those who remember the Monkey Gland.

The Morning Glory Fizz appeared for the first time in 1882 in the book by Harry Johnson, the celebrated bartender working at the time in New York. 'Fizz' qualifies a whole family of cocktails that are finished off with a little soda water (if you add more than a little you get a Collins – the nuances of the American cocktail of the period are very, very small but crucial). Since it is morning, the egg (a whole egg white) has its place in the recipe and gives it its smoothness. The absinthe is the eye-opener, but don't disregard the power of the lemon and lime juice, whose role is to activate the ailing liver. Soda or seltzer water was, of course, recommended for its medicinal effects.

All this is well and good but what really attracts us to this cocktail is the mention of Fizz, which makes everyone think of Gin Fizz. Here the base reminds us that this family can be made with every spirit imaginable (I own up to a weakness for the SeaPea – dedicated by Frank Meier to the great composer Cole Porter – whose base is exclusively absinthe). The Scotch whisky (a good blend) gives the mixture a robustness, while still retaining a certain delicacy. And if you choose one with slightly smoky notes, it can be even better. It's up to you.

**PREPARATION**

**Mix in a cocktail shaker (except for the soda water)**

**TYPE OF GLASS**

**Serve in an Old Fashioned glass, top up with soda water**

**PRESENTATION**

**Garnish with a twist of orange or lemon peel**

**DIFFICULTY**

**Difficult**

**STYLE**

**Morning-after cocktail**

**TASTE**

**Creamy, slightly aniseed, candied lemon**

**FINISH**

**Average length, but persistent smoky notes**

# 64 Mulata

INGREDIENTS

40ml (1¼ fl oz) Havana
Club 7 Años, 20ml
(¾ fl oz) Crème de cacao
(brown), 2 teaspoons
lime juice

There are eight Cuban classics in this book. This may seem a little excessive, but it's actually not that many: after the classic American mixology of the 19th century, there is no finer school than the Cuban one. Of the cocktails I have chosen, the Mulata, invented at the beginning of the 1950s, is the most recent recipe. It comes from Constante Ribalaigua's El Floridita, but dates from an era when, due to illness, he wasn't always able to be present in the bar (he died in 1952). According to Cuban sources, its creator was José Maria Vazquez, one of his pupils.

It is a cocktail of great simplicity. Take the typical Cuban base, the Daiquiri. Replace the sugar with a Crème de cacao (a good one won't be too sweet). To accompany the chocolate notes, select an older Cuban rum than you would use for a classic Daiquiri. Mix in a blender. Perfect. The texture of the blended cocktails served at the Floridita is exceptional. It's due to a little trick: the rum is not poured directly into the blender but introduced gradually, like the oil in a mayonnaise, to be blended little by little.

It should be noted that originally the Mulata was prepared in a shaker and served frappé (with crushed ice in the glass) and, importantly, Bacardi Elixir, a rum liqueur flavoured with roasted sugar cane, instead of the Crème de cacao. The authentic Elixir disappeared with the revolution and the Mulata took its modern form. Shortly after the triumph of Castro and his comrades, the bars closed, the bartenders' association was dissolved and the tourists disappeared. Chronologically, the Mulata was uncontestably the last classic of the golden age of the Cuban cocktail, which lasted nearly fifty years. The new generation is beginning to shake up Havana by night; fingers crossed that they may be able to take up the baton of Constante and all the others.

PREPARATION

**Mix in a blender**

TYPE OF GLASS

**Serve in a Martini or cocktail glass**

PRESENTATION

**Serve simply with a straw**

DIFFICULTY

**Difficult**

STYLE

**Tropical after-dinner cocktail**

TASTE

**Round, caramel and cocoa**

**FINISH**

**Slight persistent acidity, chocolate**

# 65

# Negroni

30ml (1fl oz) gin, 30ml
(1fl oz) Campari, 30ml
(1fl oz) red vermouth,
orange peel to serve
(optional)

Legend has it that one Count Camillo Negroni, a colourful character who had been a cowboy in the United States, drank a daily Americano at Florence's Caffè Casoni. One day, sometime between 1919 and 1921, he wanted to try something with more body. He suggested that Fosco Scarselli, the bartender, switch the soda water for gin.

According to another theory the Negroni was invented by a Corsican military man, but it's a tale that merits little credence. We could leave the matter there but it's appropriate to add another strange story: it took thirty years for the Negroni recipe to become established in Italy. By contrast, it was in France, where Campari had already made its mark with the Boulevardier or the Old Pal, that the three ingredients appeared together in the same cocktail, then called the Cardinale (1926). It can be found in the translation of a book by Pietro Grandi, but the bar historian Fernando Castellon states that the original edition did not include the recipe in question. This translation was sponsored by ... Campari. It would be followed in 1929 by the Camparinete, credited to Max of the Chatham Hotel.

The first Negroni (or rather Negrone) was found in Cuba in 1950, at El Floridita, as always. Of course, the publication date of a recipe is no more than an indication and the story of the Count has not been disproved by any material fact. And anyway, only one thing is really important: the Negroni is, along with the Dry Martini, the best aperitif cocktail. True, the Campari's bitterness is a bit difficult in a world that demands sweetness. Persevere a little and a whole wonderful world will open up to you. You will then understand why Italians do it bitter.

PREPARATION

**Mix directly into an Old Fashioned glass, serve over ice**

PRESENTATION

**Garnish with a twist of orange peel (optional)**

DIFFICULTY

**Easy**

STYLE

**Bitter aperitif**

TASTE

**Powerful, with notes of orange, rhubarb and herbs**

**FINISH**

**Intense and bitter without being too dry**

# 66 Old Fashioned

INGREDIENTS
..................................................
75ml (2½fl oz) American
whiskey (rye or
bourbon), 1 sugar lump,
3 dashes Angostura
bitters, lemon peel or
maraschino cherry
to serve

For years this cocktail languished in limbo. It was reserved for upper-middle-class, white American males over the age of forty. Not cool. Then came *Mad Men*, where nearly everybody is white, upper-middle class. The Old Fashioned is Don Draper's drink of choice. Very cool. And so everybody wants it but, like Don, who really knows where it came from?

Let's go back to the end of the 18th century when it was customary to use bitters (concoctions made from plant concentrates), to ease the stomach. To make the experience more palatable they were mixed with spirits, sugar and water (no ice cubes, commercial production had not yet been launched). This wound up being called a cocktail, to which quite a number of people took a liking. The mixture joined the flips, slings and grogs in the repertory of the bars of the time. Over time, the formula became increasingly sophisticated: stem glass, ice cubes to chill the mixture, the addition of liqueurs....

Then came complete mutation: during the 1880s vermouth arrived and the word 'cocktail' was used to describe the Martinez or the Manhattan. It was a small step from there to requests from clients for an 'old-fashioned cocktail': no liqueur, no pretty glass. The first recipe was published in 1888, although this can't be claimed as the date of its creation; at most it was renamed, in order to make a clear distinction between a method that had become obsolete and the new cocktails that were all the rage. Don Draper drank the primordial cocktail. And since we're talking in generic terms, while remaining faithful to the spirit of those Americans who were first to raise an elbow, it can be made with various spirits: applejack, rum, cognac, etc. The classic, however, is still made with American whiskey.

### PREPARATION

**Make directly in an Old Fashioned glass. Use a muddler to crush a lump of sugar impregnated with bitters in a little water. Gradually add the whiskey and ice cubes, stirring all the time**

### PRESENTATION

**Garnish with a twist of lemon peel or a maraschino cherry**

### DIFFICULTY

**Difficult**

### STYLE

**Powerful, primordial cocktail**

### TASTE

**Ample, with vanilla and cinnamon notes and controlled bitterness**

### FINISH

**Brief: a duel between the bitters and the sweetness of the spices**

# 67

# Paddington

INGREDIENTS
......................................

45ml (1½fl oz) Banks 5
Island rum, 15ml (½fl
oz) Lillet, 15ml (½fl oz)
grapefruit juice, 15ml
(½fl oz) lemon juice,
1 teaspoon orange
marmalade, 2 teaspoons
absinthe, grapefruit peel
to serve

In a hotdog joint in New York's East Village there's a telephone booth that calls only one number: that of the bar hidden behind it. The back of the cabin opens and you find yourself in PDT (Please Don't Tell), one of the most famous bars in the world. Although this is not the first contemporary New York speakeasy, it's the one that has defined the category and set the trend since it opened in 2007.

However, that wasn't the original idea; it occurred by chance, when the owners took advantage of the space that became available at Crif Dogs, the fast-food joint next door, without having to take out a second licence. Since then the hot dog has become an essential on the menus of trendy bars and speakeasies are even opened in countries with no history of Prohibition.

The décor of PDT includes a stuffed black bear that the team has nicknamed Paddington. Of course a cocktail had to be dedicated to him and David Slape, the first bartender hired by the director, Jim Meehan, nailed it in 2008. Ever since his debut in 1958 in the first book of the series, Michael Bond's Paddington Bear has loved orange marmalade. So that was the indispensable ingredient.

For the rest, the Paddington is reminiscent of the Corpse Reviver #2 (*see* page 62) and the Hemingway Special (*see* page 104). It's an excellent cocktail that has become inseparable from PDT, and is one of the few that features on most of their menus. In 2011 Jim Meehan published *The PDT Cocktail Book*, a landmark as much for the quality of the production as the meticulous presentation and the selection of cocktails featured. Chris Gall's illustrations are superb – if you don't want to see photos of each cocktail. Now even those outside New York can enjoy the PDT experience. Start with the Paddington.

PREPARATION

**Shake in a cocktail shaker (except for the absinthe)**

TYPE OF GLASS

**Serve in a cocktail glass previously swirled with absinthe**

PRESENTATION

**Garnish with a slice of grapefruit peel**

DIFFICULTY

**Difficult**

STYLE

**Rich, luscious cocktail**

TASTE

**Molasses, then bitter orange and aniseed**

**FINISH**

**Slight tartness, but well-balanced**

# 68 Paloma

INGREDIENTS

60ml (2fl oz) Excellia
tequila, 15ml (½fl oz)
lime juice, pinch of salt,
grapefruit soda, slice
of grapefruit or lime to
serve

These days, up-market supermarkets offer a large selection of fruit-flavoured sodas or waters. Ten years ago this was not the case. On the other hand, visitors to Mexico will know that there's a kind of tradition there: soda flavoured with watermelon, hibiscus, guava, tamarind, and so on. Jarritos, the most popular brand, was founded in 1950 and its products have thrown open the doors on a vast range of possibilities for the long drink. I don't know if Mexican bartenders really take full advantage of them but grapefruit soda has taken first place. Although we associate Mexico with the Margarita, the tipple of choice for Mexicans is reputed to be the Paloma, a blend of tequila, lime juice, salt and grapefruit soda (as with the Margarita, you can salt the rim of your glass, but it's really optional). This makes sense: weaker in alcohol, more diluted that the Margarita, the Paloma is an ideal cocktail with which to face the summer heat.

Those yet to have the pleasure of experiencing tropical summers at such close quarters should still get to know this recipe, a superb alternative to the Collinses, Mojitos or Gin & Tonics that we lazily (and automatically) prepare during hot months.

If you cannot find or are not happy with commercially made grapefruit sodas, please do not compromise on quality. Simply replace it with fresh pink grapefruit juice (90ml/3fl oz) plus 15ml (½fl oz) sugar syrup (or agave syrup) and top up with soda water. Every problem has its solution.

PREPARATION

**Mix directly in a Collins glass, serve over ice**

PRESENTATION

**Garnish with a slice of grapefruit or lime**

DIFFICULTY

**Easy**

STYLE

**Refreshing salty long drink**

TASTE

**Grapefruit, grapefruit and grapefruit, with some vegetal notes**

**FINISH**

**Medium. Very slight tartness, controlled acidity, very refreshing**

# 69

# Pegu Club

### INGREDIENTS

60ml (2fl oz) Aviation
gin, 20ml (¾fl oz)
curaçao, 15ml
(½fl oz) lime juice,
1 dash Angostura bitters,
1 dash orange bitters,
lime zest and slice to
serve

In 1943 Michael Powell and Emeric Pressburger made one of the best films in the history of British cinema: *The Life and Death of Colonel Blimp*. The lead character, a veteran of the Boer War, represents old England, the Empire on the brink of death. He has lived through the First and Second World Wars, the end of his universe, the end, as he thinks (the satire is sometimes scathing), of the sense of honour and of respectable evenings at the Gentlemen's Club.

These British institutions were exported to all of His Majesty's colonies, from Kenya to Singapore by way of India. In Burma (now Myanmar), the Pegu Club was the obligatory meeting place of all whites passing through – locals were not allowed in. Built in 1882, it welcomed Rudyard Kipling, who was struck by the conversations of the regulars, full of 'battle, murder, and sudden death'. George Orwell's *Burmese Days* (1934) paints a much darker picture of a reactionary bastion of Empire zealots, where English nobodies claimed superiority over far more intelligent Burmans. Glorious adventurers or despicable imperialists, they could all count on a well-stocked bar. And as in every gentleman's club all over the world, it had its own house cocktail.

Harry MacElhone was the first to publish the recipe in Europe, in 1927. Today Pegu Club is the name of a New York bar managed by Audrey Saunders. In Yangon (formerly Rangoon), the magnificent Pegu Club is now in ruins. The Yangon Heritage Trust is trying to restore its past splendour, along with that of many of the city's architectural treasures. It's a tough fight against property developers. Sadly, drinking a Pegu Club won't solve anything, but on the other hand, it won't bring back the Empire either. A neutral act, therefore, and as such one to be commended for the cocktail lover.

PREPARATION

**Stir in a mixing glass**

TYPE OF GLASS

**Serve in a Martini or cocktail glass**

PRESENTATION

**Garnish with lime zest and a slice of lime**

DIFFICULTY

**Moderate**

STYLE

**Aperitif for a heavy, humid day**

TASTE

**Spicy yet round; discreet citrus notes**

FINISH

Initially orange then juniper, somewhat tart

# 70

# Penicillin

### INGREDIENTS

50ml (1¾fl oz) Scotch
whisky, 20ml (¾fl oz)
lemon juice, 2 teaspoons
honey syrup, 2 teaspoons
ginger syrup, 1 teaspoon
Islay whisky, crystalized
ginger to serve

The history of alcohol begins in the world of medicine, as does the history of the cocktail. Even today, references to the pharmacopeia and the supposed curative virtues of mixed drinks continue to appear, mostly ironically. In 2013, a book on medicinal cocktails graced the shelves. I do not recommend it: mixing concepts and claiming that preparations will be good for a particular malady takes us back into the past by two centuries, which is not desirable.

Anyway, the focus is usually and more understandably on the proprieties of the herbs and plants used to make liqueurs. But medicine has evolved. One of the greatest discoveries of the 20th century was penicillin, by Alexander Fleming in 1928, which went into mass-production in 1940. It was just a matter of time before it was referenced in a cocktail. Quite logically the invention of the eponymous drink took place in New York, capital at the time (2005) of the alliance between tradition and modernity.

This alliance made its way from name to the glass: a Whiskey Sour with honey and ginger syrup. The old world of the classic cocktail discovered the potential of the fusion. The stroke of genius was to flavour the cocktail with a little peaty Islay whisky. Since then many bartenders have followed this route, whether with a whisky or a good smoky mezcal. A good idea quickly becomes commonplace but the Penicillin never disappoints. That is its strength. In the end, it is a delicious cocktail, surprising and complex. An authentic modern classic – and that's saying something, because they are not numerous – it was invented by an Australian bartender, Sam Ross, at New York's Milk & Honey. Ross still works at the same site, but in Attaboy, a new bar of which he is one of the owners.

PREPARATION

**Shake in a cocktail shaker**

TYPE OF GLASS

**Serve in an Old Fashioned glass filled with ice cubes**

PRESENTATION

**Garnish with a piece of crystallized ginger**

DIFFICULTY

**Difficult**

STYLE

**Fusion cocktail**

TASTE

**Frank and piquant (ginger), refreshing**

FINISH

**Long, peat enriched by spicy and tangy notes**

# 71

# Picon Punch

### INGREDIENTS

60ml (2fl oz) Amer Picon, 15ml (½fl oz) Merlet Brothers Blend cognac, 1 teaspoon grenadine, soda water, lemon zest and peel to serve

Some typically French products are little used in France. It used to be said in jest that more bottles of the French brand Suze were destined for Australian bars than were sold in the home market. And French consumption of cognac is ridiculously low. Picon probably saves its skin because it is drunk with beer. But the situation may be about to change thanks to the efforts of a few bartenders – recently Paris has seen the opening of two bars that use only French ingredients (À la française and Le syndicat). Will the sauce take?

At all events, in the United States Picon can be found in a number of classic cocktails, not least among them the Brooklyn, a twist on the Manhattan. Picon's bitterness and orange notes work perfectly, it's true, as an interesting alternative to the bitters of the more classic version. As for the Picon Punch, a few drops are not enough; it requires 60ml (2fl oz) of Picon, reinforced with 15ml (½ fl oz) of cognac, a little grenadine to soften it and soda water to lengthen it. But who invented this recipe? This is where it gets very strange.

It seems that Picon Punch comes from the Basque community who settled in Bakersfield, California, during the gold rush of the 1850s. Basques, Picon and California: can someone please explain? Granted, the Californians had a head start: in the 19th century they drank more Pisco (in a Pisco Punch, funnily enough) than anyone outside of Peru, and San Francisco's predilection for Fernet Branca with cola is in no way inferior to that of Buenos Aires. They're crazy, these Californians. Or, conversely, particularly sensible. You tell me.

PREPARATION

**Stir directly in a Collins glass, serve over ice**

PRESENTATION

**Garnish with lemon zest and a twist of lemon peel**

DIFFICULTY

**Easy**

STYLE

**Aperitif as a long drink**

TASTE

**Sweet and fresh, with berry-fruit notes**

FINISH

Gourmand yet herby, persistent bitter orange

# 72

# Piña Colada

## INGREDIENTS

40ml (1¼ fl oz) rum,
90ml (3 fl oz) pineapple
juice, 20ml (¾ fl
oz) coconut cream,
pineapple slice to serve

Two or three years ago the Piña Colada stood for everything that was bad about the cocktail culture of the past fifty years. Now that retro has triumphed in the world of mixology (not entirely ironically), it has made a rather enjoyable comeback. Ultimately, it's a really pleasant cocktail, a guilty pleasure, although the leap from that to a revival of Rupert Holmes's 'Escape' (known in the US as 'the Piña Colada song') is not one we want to make.

Piña Colada means 'strained pineapple'. Drinks with this name date back to the 19th century at least. But since pineapple is a fibrous fruit, the expression *piña colada* could just as easily refer to a simple pineapple juice, strained to make it more pleasant. The drink we know today was born in Puerto Rico during the 1950s. It was there that an industrial process to make coconut cream was invented in 1949 (before that it had been a difficult and lengthy artisanal job). Note that I say coconut cream, which is thicker and sweeter than the coconut milk often wrongly found in many recipes. Do not make that mistake and do not use Malibu, either in addition to or in place of the cream or (horror of horrors) the rum. Malibu is a rum-based coconut liqueur; it is too low in alcohol and tastes unsatisfactory. Once again, if you buy ready-made pineapple juice choose the best available brand and always without added sugar.

I won't pretend that this will be the most beautiful cocktail experience in this book, but it should do the trick, especially in summer or when you need to serve that rather annoying friend who doesn't really like your Penicillin.

PREPARATION

Shake in a cocktail shaker

TYPE OF GLASS

Serve in a large wine or Hurricane glass filled with ice cubes

PRESENTATION

Garnish with a pineapple slice and serve with a straw if liked

DIFFICULTY

Moderate

STYLE

Guilty tropical pleasure

TASTE

Light and unsurprising: coconut and pineapple

FINISH

Fairly brief, like the taste but with vegetal notes from the rum

# 73 Pisco Sour

## INGREDIENTS

50ml (1¾fl oz) Pisco,
30ml (1fl oz) lime juice,
30ml (1fl oz) sugar syrup,
1 egg white, 3 dashes
Angostura bitters
to serve

The family of Sours is ecumenical and accepts all kinds of spirits. One of the most exotic is the still under-utilized Pisco. Like cognac, it is a wine distillate, but it is not matured in oak casks. This gives a light, floral eau-de-vie with sufficient character to serve as the base for a cocktail. Both Chile and Peru claim the paternity of Pisco. I don't want to create a diplomatic incident, so will confine myself to talking about our recipe, which is incontrovertibly of Peruvian origin.

Victor Morris, an American who lived in Peru for many years, is often credited with popularizing the drink. As with the Daiquiri, it's reasonable to suggest it was being made before this, in fact a similar recipe appeared in a 1903 cookbook, well before Morris. In Peru there are four types of Pisco, each with its own properties: the Puro (a single variety of grape, non-aromatic), the Aromática (a single variety, aromatic), the Mosto Verde (distilled from partially fermented must) and the Acholado (blended from several grape varieties). Each will have an impact on the final taste but, so long as the brand is of good quality, they will all give you a good cocktail – it is not as if the resulting mixture is particularly demanding as to the particularities of the spirit.

You should be aware that the lime available in Peru is not the same as the one generally found over here (Persian lime): it's related to the lime found in the Antilles. Consequently some bartenders use a mixture of lemon and lime juice. I won't make any recommendations but will leave you with the opportunity to experiment. Finally, egg white is really essential in this Sour, although a few drops of bitters should be added to the white surface of your cocktail. You could try making a small pattern but it is the flavour that matters.

PREPARATION

**Shake in a cocktail shaker (except the Angostura)**

TYPE OF GLASS

**Pour into a cocktail or Old Fashioned glass**

PRESENTATION

**Garnish with dashes of Angostura**

DIFFICULTY

**Moderate**

STYLE

**Floral and tangy aperitif**

TASTE

**Silky, grape must subdued by the sugar**

**FINISH**

**Light and subtle, perfectly balanced**

# Planter's Punch

60ml (2fl oz) Jamaican rum, 30ml (1fl oz) lime juice, 15ml (½fl oz) grenadine, 3 dashes Angostura bitters, soda water, 1 mint sprig to serve

In the history of what is now called the cocktail, punch features as a precursor. Brought back from the Orient by the sailors of the East India Company, it became popular in 17th-century London. The debate remains open as to whether it was the invention of idle sailors or a local drink but, like the expert David Wondrich, I tend towards the first theory. It is said that the name derives from the Hindu word for five, the number of ingredients: alcohol, water (or tea), spices, sugar and the juice of a citrus fruit. After the first sip, and especially after the intoxicating effect (see Hogarth's illustrations on this subject, they are almost psychedelic), the English took it everywhere, particularly to the sugar plantations of the Caribbean, where Planter's Punch first emerged.

I understand their penchant: a hostile climate, no modern comforts and having to spend all day mistreating slaves – no wonder they were driven to drink! You can be sure that there were as many recipes for Planter's Punch as there were planters, just as today there are countless different recipes – often, it must be said, undrinkable ones. Ours, which has become a classic, comes from Jamaica, and even if it leaves out all the classic paraphernalia of punch (the pretty bowl, the silver ladle, the little glasses) and all the details of its meticulous preparation (the production of oleo-saccharum, that is to say steeping lemon zest in sugar and then leaving it for several hours to draw out the oils), it respects the spirit.

Soda water, Jamaican rum, lime juice, syrup of grenadine and Angostura (for the spices): we have our five ingredients. Whether you are sitting on a porch with a view over the cane-fields or in an attic room in a provincial town, a change of scene is guaranteed, but without the barbarous and inhumane practices or the risk of yellow fever.

PREPARATION

Mix directly into a Collins or an Old Fashioned glass, serve over crushed ice

PRESENTATION

Garnish with a sprig of mint

DIFFICULTY

Easy

STYLE

Refreshing long drink

TASTE

Fruity and slightly sharp, easy-drinking

FINISH

Slightly bitter, the rum evident but moderated by the fruit and sugar

# 75

## Porto Flip

90ml (3fl oz) port,
2 teaspoons sugar syrup,
1 whole egg, grated
nutmeg to serve

Do you remember General Harrison's Egg Nogg? I mentioned in this context the Flip, 'a mixture of beer, rum, sugar and egg into which was plunged a red-hot poker to heat it', which later became a drink for 'delicate persons'. Here is one of these famous, more sophisticated versions: goodbye to the beer, farewell to the rum and hello to fortified wine. Sherry and Madeira, which were much in demand in the US throughout the 19th century, of course took place of honour, especially among consumers of a certain socio-economic bracket.

This is explained by the fact that sherry and madeira are among those rare wines able to stand up to a long voyage and they had the cachet (and the price) of imported goods. So they had everything going for them. Let us turn to another fortified wine: port. Before the American Civil War, it was extremely popular in Sangaree, a drink imported from the UK, which a Flip slightly resembles. Unlike its rough and ready predecessor, it is served cold with sugar and garnished with nutmeg.

Obviously this is still a Flip and so a whole egg is used. It needs to be well shaken because you want a perfect emulsion. In addition to fortified wines, a Flip can also be made with many different spirits (from cognac to rum by way of apple brandy or whisky). The port Flip seems to me particularly balanced and elegant (with its amazing colour), perfect for a long winter evening. If you opt instead for sherry, the amount of wine remains the same but the quantity of sugar needs to be adjusted, depending on whether you choose an Amontillado or an Oloroso, for example. On the other hand, if you are looking for bigger thrills and plump for spirits, don't forget to reduce the quantity of alcohol (to around 60ml/2fl oz maximum).

PREPARATION

**Shake in a cocktail shaker (see left)**

TYPE OF GLASS

**Serve in a small wine glass or in a Champagne flute**

PRESENTATION

**Garnish with freshly grated nutmeg**

DIFFICULTY

**Moderate**

STYLE

**Delicate winter cocktail**

TASTE

**Red fruits, very creamy, milky aromas**

FINISH

**Slightly sugary and tannic, notes of cacao rather than coffee**

# 76 El Presidente

INGREDIENTS
.........................................

45ml (1½fl oz) Havana
Club 3 Años, 45ml
(1½fl oz) Dolin vermouth
de Chambéry blanc,
1 teaspoon curaçao,
½ teaspoon grenadine,
orange peel to serve

Ah, the Presidente! You will find it made with an aged rum when what it really needs is a young Cuban one. You will find it made with fruit juice when it should boast a little liqueur. You will find it made with red or dry vermouth instead of Chambéry. Chambéry vermouth, really? Yes, and the top choice comes from Dolin, the 1821 creator of the category and its distinctive style, imitated by other producers. The world's best-selling vermouth, Martini Bianco, is just one of many imitations of Chambéry, but most of these imitators never quite manage to achieve the finesse and quality of the pioneering product.

The now defunct Comoz brand brought Chambéry vermouth to Cuba around 1907. It rapidly became a favourite of Cuban bartenders, as its less bitter, more floral profile suited the local palate. Mixed with their national light rum, it gave birth to the second Cuban classic, after the Daiquiri. Don't believe all the stories that attribute this recipe to various Americans who arrived after Prohibition in 1920. El Presidente was already in the very first book on Cuban cocktails published in 1915 by one John Escalante. Fernando Castellon discovered this in 2013 in Cuba's National Library.

No doubt Escalante, like many Cuban *cantineros*, was Spanish (and his real first name was probably Juan). There are some indications that before arriving in Cuba he spent some time in New York, where he may have learned the fundamentals of the trade, but it is hard to know if he invented this cocktail. The honoured president in question was Mario Garcia Menocal, an engineer who was elected in May 1913. The recipe changed over the run of presidents and the years. This recipe was the standard during the 1920s. Light, aromatic, elegant: all the beauty of the Cuban cocktail.

**PREPARATION**

**Stir in a mixing glass**

**TYPE OF GLASS**

**Serve in a Martini or cocktail glass**

**PRESENTATION**

**Garnish with a twist of orange peel**

**DIFFICULTY**

**Moderate**

**STYLE**

**Sweet aperitif**

**TASTE**

**Round, slightly sugary, delicately fruity**

**FINISH**

**Persistent sweetness, over molasses and floral notes**

# 77

# Prince of Wales

## INGREDIENTS

45ml (1½fl oz) rye whiskey, 2 teaspoons sugar syrup, 1 dash maraschino liqueur, 1 dash Angostura bitters, 1 small piece of fresh pineapple, 30ml (1fl oz) brut Champagne, lemon slice to serve

The cocktail was originally developed in a very specific environment, composed of students, journalists, lawyers, artists, gamblers, womanizers and, of course, drinkers. They were known as 'sportsmen' and represented the Rabelaisian side of America: '*fay ce que vouldras*' ('do what you will'). In Europe at the same period, the profile was socially more distinct; it was generally the idle sons of the aristocracy who could indulge such passions.

The most prominent among them was undoubtedly Albert Edward of Saxe-Coburg-Gotha, Queen Victoria's son and heir. The flighty lover of actresses and fine bottles, he was the target of much gossip. When he finally acceded to the throne in 1901 (at nearly 60), an American publisher issued *The Private Life of King Edward VII*, written 'by a member of the Royal household'. Barely three days after the death of his mother a copy was deposited at the Library of Congress, which indicates that the publisher had sniffed a hit. In it can be found this splendid recipe, which Bertie might have invented during one of his many visits to the United States, country of liberty and long-legged chorus-girls where, one imagines, his activities were less strictly monitored than at home.

A cocktail in the classic sense of the term, to which a piece of pineapple is added, it is, importantly, topped off with Champagne. It's a sort of Champagne Old Fashioned served straight up. Surprising and delicious. Of course, this is not a stroke of princely genius: according to the cocktail historian David Wondrich, adding Champagne was a fashion of the 1880s (even in a Manhattan) – 'it was the best of times, it was the worst of times', as someone said elsewhere. Whatever the case, this time the inspiration was royal.

**PREPARATION**

**Shake in a cocktail shaker (except the Champagne)**

**TYPE OF GLASS**

**Serve in a cocktail glass or Champagne coupe and top up with Champagne**

**PRESENTATION**

**Garnish with a slice of lemon**

**DIFFICULTY**

**Moderate**

**STYLE**

**Royal aperitif**

**TASTE**

**Freshness and effervescence, the Champagne dominates**

**FINISH**

Spices and herbs, with a light persistent sharpness

163

# 78

# Queen's Park Swizzle

## INGREDIENTS

90ml (3fl oz) Demerara rum, 20ml (¾fl oz) lime juice, 15ml (½fl oz) Demerara sugar syrup, 3 dashes Angostura bitters, 10 mint leaves plus an extra sprig to serve

The Bombacaceae family includes not only the baobab (whose fruit, by the way, is used in the distillation of Whitley Neill gin). There is also the *Quararibea turbinate*, a tree found almost everywhere in the Antilles. It is also known as the swizzle-stick tree, as its branches were used to make the famous little five- or three-pronged baton traditionally used to stir certain dishes and drinks. As its Latin name indicates, it slightly resembles a turbine (not a nuclear one, although this cocktail might give the lie to that). From the 18th century onwards this small baton, aka swizzle stick, gave its name to a family of cocktails originally made with rum – although nowadays one finds more and more recipes that turn their back on this tradition (*see* the Chartreuse Swizzle, page 58).

Among those that respect their heritage, I am particularly fond of the Queen's Park Swizzle, which was probably born in Port of Spain, capital of Trinidad and Tobago and home to the Queen's Park Savannah and Hotel, founded in 1893. Most Swizzles take the classic formula: rum, lime juice and syrup. The Queen's Park is distinguished by a good dose of Angostura bitters, the pride of the island. Although the mixture originated in Venezuela, production moved from there to Trinidad and Tobago in 1875. The rum is not local. With a base of molasses made from Demerara sugar and produced in British Guyana, it has great character and makes its mark. The mint adds the finishing touch.

To 'swizzle' your cocktail, add all the ingredients and fill the glass with ice. With the swizzle stick fully immersed in the depth of the glass, place the end between your palms and rotate it rapidly by rubbing your hands forwards and backwards. Continue until fully mixed and the rim of the glass is frosted.

PREPARATION

**Mix directly in a Collins glass, serve over crushed ice**

PRESENTATION

**Garnish with a sprig of mint (optional)**

DIFFICULTY

**Difficult**

STYLE

**Tropical refreshment**

TASTE

**Powerful, with Demerara sugar and spices**

FINISH

Long and complex, rum dominating

# 79

# Ramos Gin Fizz

### INGREDIENTS

40ml (1¼fl oz) Old Tom
gin, ½ tablespoon sugar,
2 teaspoons lemon juice,
2 teaspoons lime juice,
3 drops orange flower
water, 1 egg white, 30ml
(1fl oz) single cream,
soda water, orange slice
to serve (optional)

In 1915, during Mardi Gras, a visitor to the New Orleans's Stag Saloon came upon a scene that defied comprehension: 35 young boys whose sole task was to shake as hard and for as long as possible the shakers that a bartender passed to them, the reason being that the cocktail in question was very popular and required a lengthy and vigorous shake. It combined fresh cream and egg white in an era bereft of any electrical device to speed up the operation (nowadays a milk frother would achieve more than the efforts of all the young boys in the world).

The Ramos Gin Fizz – the name by which it passed into history, having long been known as the New Orleans Fizz – was invented at the end of the 19th century by Henry C. Ramos, a bartender of German origin who, after operating saloons in Baton-Rouge (Louisiana) and Birmingham (Alabama), set up in New Orleans around 1888. There he opened the Imperial Cabinet, in the very spot where Joseph Santini (*see* page 49) had operated his Parlor a few years earlier. In 1907 Ramos took over the Stag, a bigger bar situated opposite the prestigious St Charles Hotel. His cocktail is a kind of baroque Fizz: as if the egg white and cream did not suffice, Ramos mixed two kinds of juice and added – the secret ingredient – a few drops of orange flower water. Properly prepared, it is velvety, creamy, unbelievably satisfying. 'It's like drinking a flower', exclaimed one enraptured client. And it's perfect for brunch.

That would have pleased Ramos, who detested drunks and closed his bar every evening at 8pm, after the aperitif hour. In the same spirit, I propose a recipe less strong in alcohol. The exact formula was a well-guarded secret. Then Prohibition arrived and the business closed, so Ramos passed his drink on for the benefit of future generations. God bless him.

**PREPARATION**

Mix in a cocktail shaker (except for the soda water)

**TYPE OF GLASS**

Serve in a small wine glass and top up with a little soda water

**PRESENTATION**

Garnish with a slice of orange (optional)

**DIFFICULTY**

Difficult

**STYLE**

Creamy brunch cocktail

**TASTE**

Very silky and sweet

**FINISH**

Orange flower and creamy

# 80 Rio Bravo

50ml (1¾fl oz) cachaça,
20ml (¾fl oz) lime juice,
15ml (½fl oz) orgeat
(almond syrup), 3 slices
ginger, orange zest and a
slice of peel to serve

Every book has its faults, and the least of this collection's is to present so few cocktails based on cachaça, that Brazilian cousin of agricultural rum. In a mood of provocation, I could justify myself by asking the following question: does the world really need another Caipirinha recipe? The problem with cachaça and cocktails is that there is no other classic.

Poorly understood and little loved, cachaça emerged from obscurity only relatively recently. It was chiefly only very creative bartenders, skilled in the gourmet craft of the cocktail, who took an interest in it. Some excellent recipes were created but they often included one or another esoteric ingredient that made trying the recipes complicated for those without access to a bar where they were offered. Until there is a more accessible cocktail concept, we will not have a genuine modern cachaça-based classic. This may be a pity but it is another reason to visit your favourite (good) bar. If it is up to scratch you may find there some excellent artisanal cachaça such as Engenho da Vertente. Better-known brands such as Sagatiba also work very well in cocktails.

Having said all this, Nidal Ramini comes to our rescue with a cocktail that is both familiar (a Sour, yet again) and different, thanks to the cachaça, orgeat and ginger, which should be muddled in the shaker. In London bars such as Dusk and then Montgomery Place, Ramini has been one of the kingpins of the capital's magnificent cocktail scene over the past ten years. He also gave some of today's best bartenders, such as Ago Perrone (to be found in the Connaught Hotel, London) or Giuseppe Santamaria (at Ohla, in Barcelona) their chance too. Plus he also has, if the name of his recipe does not deceive me, good taste in movies....

PREPARATION

**Shake in a cocktail shaker (see left)**

TYPE OF GLASS

**Serve in a cocktail glass**

PRESENTATION

**Garnish with orange zest and a slice of peel**

DIFFICULTY

**Difficult**

STYLE

**Refreshing, spicy cocktail**

TASTE

**Cane juice, spicy, little touch of lemongrass**

FINISH

**Medium, the lemon cleans the palate, lingering ginger**

# 81 Rose

40ml (1¼fl oz) kirsch,
20ml (¾fl oz) dry
vermouth, 2 teaspoons
Cherry Heering,
1 maraschino cherry
to serve

From the end of the 19th century until World War II, the Opera quarter of Paris was the centre of the American community and therefore of cocktail bars. People went to Henry's at the Hotel Scribe, or to the Cecil before slumming it in Pigalle. Nowadays all that remains is Harry's New York Bar. Just a few metres from this legendary establishment was the Chatham Hotel, where Johnny Mitta officiated at the beginning of the 20th century.

He created the Rose, a cocktail as delicate as it is delicious, which combines dry vermouth and kirsch (it is essential to use a quality kirsch, cheap products are absolutely undrinkable). The earliest recipes, published in the 1920s, do not agree on the proportions: some specify more vermouth, others more kirsch. Sometimes a little gooseberry syrup or cherry brandy was added on the side, or on occasion both. By 1929 the book *Cocktail de Paris* already featured no fewer than seven different recipes, sponsored by the venerable Cherry Rocher brand. As Robert Vermeire summed up in 1938 in *L'art du cocktail* (the very rare French version of his book *Cocktails: How to Mix Them*), 'it is never made in the same way anywhere'. Before, of course, offering 'his' version: dry vermouth, dry sherry, cherry brandy and a little Crème de cassis. And today at PDT in New York they use a spoonful of raspberry jam.

Like Vermeire's, their version is not at all bad but I suggest leaving jams or syrups aside on a first encounter with this beautiful, often overlooked concoction. The recipe here is devised by Fernando Castellon. It's a superb aperitif. It should not be confused with the Rose Cocktail, an English invention, created during World War I by Syd Knight at the Cecil Hotel. A sort of perfect Martini, like many that were 'invented' during the period.

PREPARATION

**Stir in a mixing glass**

TYPE OF GLASS

**Serve in a cocktail glass**

PRESENTATION

**Garnish with a maraschino cherry**

DIFFICULTY

**Moderate**

STYLE

**Dry, light aperitif**

TASTE

**Slightly piquant and herby, with a touch of citrus**

FINISH

**Brief, on the cherry with some almond notes**

# 82 Rubicon

INGREDIENTS

60ml (2fl oz) gin,
15ml (½fl oz) green
Chartreuse, 15ml
(½fl oz) maraschino
liqueur, 15ml (½fl oz)
lemon juice, 1 sprig
rosemary to serve

Jamie Boudreau has acquired a certain reputation in the field of molecular mixology (foams, cocktails in caviar, etc.), but he is also a great connoisseur of the traditional cocktail and an excellent communicator: his video series 'Raising the Bar', available free on the Internet, reveals his skill at finding tricks that add a little something extra to the homemade cocktail. You will learn more about technical questions there than in reading this book. If you ever pass through Seattle, say Hi to him at Canon, the place he opened in 2011 that has made him talked about – and not only for his 'Angostura-coloured' bar.

In 2007, he created an excellent cocktail that will delight your friends both with its taste and its looks: the Rubicon. At its heart are green Chartreuse and rosemary. The problem with rosemary is that, unlike basil, you cannot simply put it in the shaker and muddle it to extract the taste. Boudrea's solution is simple: place the rosemary in the bottom of the glass, pour over the Chartreuse (and its 55 per cent ABV) and flame the lot – but not for too long. The remaining ingredients, previously chilled in the shaker, are poured onto the flames, which they will extinguish. Top up with crushed ice.

All this looks easy, but on a first attempt you may well leave the rosemary burning too long. Don't be discouraged: the game is worth the candle (as it were). As well as giving a slightly smoky touch and bringing out all the aromatic notes of the rosemary, this technique intensifies the herbal element of the Chartreuse. The lemon provides a welcome contrast. Rosemary smoking is now a widespread practice, like aromatization with a peaty whisky or a mescal (*see* the Penicillin, page 148). This also works very well in recipes with tequila.

PREPARATION

**Shake in a cocktail shaker (see left)**

TYPE OF GLASS

**Serve in an Old Fashioned glass and top up with crushed ice**

PRESENTATION

**Garnish with a sprig of rosemary**

DIFFICULTY

**Difficult**

STYLE

**Herbaceous cocktail**

TASTE

**Complex, bitter and lemony, pine**

**FINISH**

**Average length, juniper and herbs**

# Saint-Germain-des-Prés

40ml (1¼ fl oz) Hendrick's gin, 20ml (¾ fl oz) lime juice, 20ml (¾ fl oz) Belvoir elderflower cordial, 20ml (¾ fl oz) St Germain elderflower liqueur, 4 dashes Scrappy's Firewater bitters, egg white, slice cucumber to serve

It would be unfair to attribute the comeback of the cocktail in a particular city to a single bar. Even during their darkest hours the leading capitals of the world still retained a couple of bars in which one could drink well. However, the impact of well-planned initiatives should not be underestimated. In Paris, the 2007 launch of the Experimental Cocktail Club marked a significant moment: smart decor, ambiance aimed at a young clientele, modern cocktails. It was New York in Paris and the venture was an immediate success.

Romée de Goriainoff, Olivier Bon and Pierre-Charles Cros, the three partners in the Expé, now run more than ten bars around the world (including the Beef Club, the Curio Parlor and the Prescription, in Paris). To maintain standards and to avoid joining the list of trendy bars to disappear after two years, first-class staff are key, and if they don't already exist they need to be trained. Logically, these new bartenders then spread their wings and open their own bars. The Expé had played a fundamental role in the explosion of the French capital's offering. Just take a walk around the fashionable bars and consider where the bartenders have come from.

One of the best-selling cocktails is the Saint-Germain-des-Prés, created as Nico's Gimlet by Nico De Soto when he worked in Canada. De Soto then spent some time in various of the group's bars and is now internationally recognized as one of the world's best bartenders – in 2014 his peers elected him best in France. This cocktail should be prepared with a tincture of Thai chillies, but these can be replaced with spicy bitters, which are more readily available. You could also try (at your own risk and peril) putting a chilli in the shaker. The cucumber should be muddled in the bottom of the shaker.

PREPARATION

**Shake in a cocktail shaker (*see left*)**

TYPE OF GLASS

**Serve in a cocktail glass**

PRESENTATION

**Garnish with a thin slice of cucumber**

DIFFICULTY

**Difficult**

STYLE

**Spring cocktail**

TASTE

**Silky, very slightly spicy; notes of lychee and citrus**

FINISH

Lingering spiciness but not too intense; lychee and cucumber

# 84 Sangrita

INGREDIENTS

30ml (1 fl oz) fresh
orange juice, 20ml
(¾ fl oz) lime juice, 15ml
(½ fl oz) grenadine,
3 dashes Tabasco sauce,
tequila to serve

Blanco, reposado or añejo, tequila is becoming increasingly popular with connoisseurs. As always, certain rules should be followed to make it an ideal experience, the key one being to reject anything that is not 100 per cent agave (i.e. all the liquid should be distilled from the fermented juice of the blue agave). Forget mixtures that blend agave and a distillate of other kinds of sugars (you will find this information on the label). Next, it's up to you to choose a bottle using your palate as your guide, and your wallet – genuine tequilas are not always cheap.

Unfortunately, some consumers still have nightmare memories of student days, involving shots of tequila, salt and a slice of lime, and are wary of approaching a decent bottle. I went through that phase. If this is also the case for you, do make an effort to discover the vegetable and earthy notes of the great tequilas. A good way to re-educate the penitent shot-drinker is to drink tequila as they do in Mexico, accompanied by a glass of sangrita, a mixture of orange and lime juice, grenadine and a spicy sauce. Not tomato juice, however: this is not the base for a Mexican Bloody Mary.

The recipe here comes from Jeffrey Morgenthaler, who was looking for an easily made version for those who, like most of us, do not have ready (or inexpensive) access to Seville oranges and to the genuine pomegranate juice of 'authentic' recipes (in as much as that word has any real meaning). You can have a pleasant-tasting cocktail, gently alternating a little sangrita, a sip of tequila. This should help you to pass the first stage of the rehabilitation programme. Next, try a reposado. On its own.

PREPARATION

**Stir in a mixing glass**

TYPE OF GLASS

**Serve in a glass of your choice**

PRESENTATION

**Accompany with a 50ml (1¾ fl oz) glass of tequila**

DIFFICULTY

**Easy**

STYLE

**Tequila's fellow traveller**

TASTE

**Slightly acid, berry fruits, spicy**

**FINISH**

**Medium spicy and notes of pomegranate**

# 85 Sazerac

INGREDIENTS

60ml (2fl oz) rye whiskey,
2 teaspoons sugar syrup,
4 dashes Peychaud's
bitters, ½ teaspoon
Pernod absinthe, lemon
peel to serve

They say many things about the Sazerac, most of them false. It's not the world's oldest cocktail – recipes in this style didn't appear before the 1850s, fifty years after the 'official' debut of the American cocktail. Consequently, the word cocktail does not come from the eggcup (*coquetier* in French) that the pharmacist Antoine Peychaud might have used to measure out the drink's ingredients. Peychaud probably did not invent the Sazerac either, even if he did create the bitters that bear his name (an essential ingredient in its makeup, although alternatives have recently appeared).

But what is a Sazerac? Initially it was the name of a cognac distiller, Sazerac de Forge et Fils, and subsequently a bar, Sazerac House, run by the official importer of Sazerac cognacs. You might think, therefore, that this was where the Sazerac was invented – as a brandy-based 'house recipe'. But the phylloxera aphid put paid to that, changing the course of history when it arrived in Cognac in 1872.

Ravaged vineyards, production in free fall, so cognac no longer reached New Orleans. The city's bars had to fall back on another spirit, one popular with the Anglo-Saxons who had begun to dominate the city: rye whiskey. The Sazerac House obviously did the same and its house cocktail changed its base spirit. In fact, the first Sazerac recipe was not published until 1908 in San Francisco and there is nothing to lend weight to the brandy theory. According to the historian David Wondrich, the Sazerac has always been made with whisky. In 1912, the banned absinthe disappeared in favour of Herbsaint, a local substitute. Today you have a choice: Sazerac with whiskey, with cognac or a mixture of the two. Whether it's historic or not, it's always a success.

**PREPARATION**

**Stir in a mixing glass, except for the absinthe**

**TYPE OF GLASS**

**Serve in an Old Fashioned glass previously swirled with the absinthe**

**PRESENTATION**

**Express some lemon peel over the surface and serve with a twist of peel**

**DIFFICULTY**

**Difficult**

**STYLE**

**Strong, complex cocktail**

**TASTE**

**Complex and spicy, perfectly balanced between bitterness and sugar**

**FINISH**

**Round, aniseed, slight dryness**

# 86 Scofflaw

## INGREDIENTS

45ml (1½ fl oz)
rye whiskey, 30ml
(1fl oz) dry vermouth,
20ml (¾fl oz) lemon
juice, 15ml (½fl oz)
grenadine, lemon
peel to serve

We are always hearing about the speed of the information age, of the immediacy of a world that our grandparents never knew. And yet, if you look at the following chronology, you might be surprised at the speed of our forebears: on 16 January 1924 the *Boston Herald* announced the result of a competition to invent a name for people who continued to drink despite Prohibition; on 27 January the *Chicago Tribune* announced that a Parisian bartender had invented a cocktail bearing this (new) name. It took just 11 days to create a word and cocktail that are both still with us, and for both to make a round-trip across the Atlantic. Without the Internet. Beat that.

In fact, the word Scofflaw had already been used a few months earlier by the writer Walt Mason, without anybody noticing (except, perhaps, the winners of the contest). The Scofflaw is therefore one of those cocktails that mocked the American 'noble' experiment. In this context I will mention the Three Mile Limit, 'commemorating' the distance from the US coastline beyond which it was legal to drink, and its little brother the Twelve Mile Limit, born when the authorities persuaded other nations to give them a little more space for water, nothing but water.

You won't be surprised to learn that the Scofflaw originated in that haunt of thirsty Americans in exile, Harry's New York Bar in Paris. It was much easier to make fun of the Prohibitionist frenzy from the safety of Europe, so this is another 'Prohibition' cocktail that was neither invented in a speakeasy, nor in the United States. Perhaps its creator was not even American – we only know his first name, Jock, the Scottish diminutive of John. In any case his cocktail got him talked about and, while it is less often prepared than it was a few decades ago, it won't do you any harm, whether you scoff at the law or not.

**PREPARATION**

**Shake in a cocktail shaker**

**TYPE OF GLASS**

**Serve in a cocktail glass**

**PRESENTATION**

**Garnish with a twist of lemon peel**

**DIFFICULTY**

**Moderate**

**STYLE**

**Law-mocking cocktail**

**TASTE**

**Round and gourmand, gingerbread and berry fruits**

**FINISH**

**Medium, balanced, unexpectedly dry; whiskey dominates**

# 87 Serendipity

20ml (¾fl oz) Calvados,
50ml (1¾fl oz) clear
apple juice, 2 teaspoons
caster sugar, 3 sprigs of
mint plus extra to serve,
75ml (2½fl oz) brut
Champagne, mint sprig
to serve

We've already mentioned a number of bars and bartenders of Europe's golden age of the cocktail, which ran from the beginning of the 1920s to the end of the 1930s. And we've already drawn your attention to several great names in the current, welcome renaissance. But it would be wrong and, importantly, insulting to pretend that a veritable desert reigned between the two eras. Dick Bradsell in England and Charles Schumann in Germany knew how to keep things alive.

In France, Colin Field is one of the bartenders skilled at maintaining the old values. Since 1994 he has presided over the Hemingway Bar at the Hotel Ritz, Paris. A Francophile Englishman, he created in the same year a true modern classic that he presents as 'France in a glass'. The drink consists of apple juice, brut Champagne and, above all, Calvados, a spirit unjustly relegated in France to the category of 'granddad's hooch', whereas it is one of the finest French products in existence.

A 'good Calva' is every bit as good as a fine cognac and it is sad that the general public will often serve it only to flambé their desserts – and that producers are unable to find a more original way of promoting it than the uninteresting Calvados and tonic. Colin Field's great merit is to offer it in a first-class creation sold in an equally first-class setting, challenging some unfortunate beliefs. He has used one of the most beautiful words in the English language to name this very French cocktail and we hope that many of his clients have had the happy surprise of rediscovering the beauty of Calvados. Crush the mint, juice and sugar with a muddler before adding the ice cubes and calvados, then stir. Top up with the Champagne.

PREPARATION

**Stir directly in a Collins glass, except for the Champagne (see left), serve over ice cubes and top up with the Champagne**

PRESENTATION

**Garnish with a sprig of mint**

DIFFICULTY

**Difficult**

STYLE

**Refreshing long drink**

TASTE

**Light effervescence, fruity and refreshing**

FINISH

**Brief but elegant, apple comes out**

# 88 Sherry Cobbler

INGREDIENTS
.......................................

120ml (4fl oz)
Amontillado sherry,
2 teaspoons caster sugar,
3 orange slices, 1 cherry
to serve

What was 19th-century America's most popular drink? The Whiskey Cocktail? The Mint Julep? The Manhattan? The answer is the Sherry Cobbler. As already mentioned, from Madeira to port, fortified wines were greatly appreciated in the United States. Wine, too: Punch gradually gave way to the Cup, especially made with red Bordeaux. The lighter alcoholic strength was better suited to the new industrial world than the Punches so beloved of sailors and planters. Cobblers can be made with all these ingredients (and even with spirits, incidentally) but a special place was reserved for sherries, the splendid, many-faceted fortified wines long relegated by ignorance to the level of a tipple for elderly ladies. But what is a Cobbler?

It couldn't be simpler: put a little sugar and several slices of orange in a cocktail shaker; add 120ml (4fl oz) of the base of your choice (less if it's a spirit). Shake well with ice cubes (if they are large, break them up with the back of a spoon). Serve in a glass without straining and garnish with seasonal berries. The beauty is in the simplicity. According to historians, the Sherry Cobbler came into being with the development of the ice industry and required the use of a new gadget, the straw. Perhaps even more than the delicious taste of the mixture, it was these two novelties that captivated the contemporary imagination and brought American mixed drinks to the global market.

At the 1867 World's Fair in Paris, the Sherry Cobbler wowed the Parisians; it was said that the American Bar got through 500 bottles of sherry a day (used to make more than 3,500 cobblers). Our ancestors were no fools; try it for yourself. The recipe I suggest is calibrated for a dry sherry. Adjust the quantity of sugar according to the sherry you choose.

**PREPARATION**

Shake in a cocktail shaker (see left)

**TYPE OF GLASS**

Serve in an Old Fashioned glass

**PRESENTATION**

Garnish with a cherry and the orange slices

**DIFFICULTY**

Difficult

**STYLE**

Refreshing old-style cocktail

**TASTE**

At first sweet and orangey, mineral thereafter

**FINISH**

Long, notes of raisin and orange

# 89 Sidecar

40ml (1¼fl oz) Merlet
Brothers Blend cognac,
20ml (¾fl oz) Merlet
triple sec, 2 teaspoons
lemon juice, lemon slice
to serve

Contrary to what one hears (especially at Harry's New York Bar in Paris), neither Harry MacElhone nor his bartenders invented the Sidecar. There really is no debate about this, since in his *ABC of Mixing Cocktails* in 1922 (not 1919, as often said) as well as in *Barflies and Cocktails* (1927), Harry himself attributes this cocktail to Pat McGarry, bartender at Buck's Club in London, where they were probably colleagues. Robert Vermeire also credits McGarry with the introduction of the cocktail to London in 1922, although he writes that the drink was popular in the south of France. Had McGarry been a bartender on the Riviera or is the creator yet another, third, person? We know no more.

The story that the name came from a soldier who got around in a sidecar is highly likely to be apocryphal. Of course nobody would fight to be credited with a dud cocktail, and the Sidecar is one of the great classics of the art of mixology. Its roots go back a long way: think of the Brandy Crusta (*see* page 48), or the Brandy Daisy, a mixture of cognac, lemon juice, sugar and a little rum, topped up with soda water (delicious, try to find the recipe, you won't regret it). The creator of the Sidecar, whether McGarry or A.N. Other, adapted that base to the tastes of his time, so it was goodbye to the curaçao and hello to the triple sec (Cointreau is specified in all historic recipes, but brands such as Combier or Merlet also give good results). This was the recipe that began to predominate in cocktail bars, and it also has the advantage of being lighter.

The recipe is simplified and limited to its three characteristic ingredients (originally in equal proportions). My palate is tired of the Sidecar, but it remains an indispensable classic that will please many enthusiasts.

**PREPARATION**

Shake in a cocktail shaker

**TYPE OF GLASS**

Serve in a cocktail glass, rim frosted with sugar (optional, *see* page 218)

**PRESENTATION**

Garnish with a slice of lemon

**DIFFICULTY**

Moderate

**STYLE**

Orangey digestif

**TASTE**

Orange, orange and orange

**FINISH**

The cognac supports the orange tamed by the lemon

# 90 Southside

INGREDIENTS
.................................
60ml (2fl oz) Citadelle
gin, 30ml (1fl oz) lime
juice, 20ml (¾fl oz) sugar
syrup, 1 sprig
mint to serve

The Southside has lived many lives, and acquired many recipes and stories, two of which relate to the Prohibition era. The first is that this cocktail originated in Chicago, where it was the preferred tipple of the gangsters of the South Side, the stamping ground of Johnny Torrio and Al Capone. Another recipe refers to New York's legendary 21 Club, a luxurious speakeasy founded in 1929, where the owners installed an ingenious system that enabled them to tip the liquor bottles and their contents through a chute and into the city's sewers in the event of a police raid. (The 21 still exists, but it is now a respectable restaurant and favourite lunch spot of American presidents.)

Both of these theories are credible: poor-quality gin was common and lime juice, sugar and mint are ideal to disguise shortcomings. According to the journalist Eric Felten, the cocktail actually came from the Southside Sportmen's Club. Funnily enough, this very exclusive club was based in Long Island, close to the home of a certain Gatsby, bootlegger extraordinaire, and one can imagine his guests delighting in it (even if his creator F. Scott Fitzgerald preferred a Gin Rickey – without sugar or mint).

Back to the recipes: while lime juice has become the standard, older recipes mention lemon juice. Should it be served in a stemmed glass or one filled with ice cubes and topped up with soda water? We see them all. I have decided to propose what may be a base recipe. You can prepare it as such and serve it in a cocktail glass: fantastic. You can serve it in an Old Fashioned glass and add a little soda water: fantastic. Or in a tall glass filled with ice cubes and topped up with soda water: fantastic. Three cocktails for the price of one. No speakeasy, then or now, would offer you such a good deal.

**PREPARATION**

Shake in a cocktail shaker

**TYPE OF GLASS**

Serve in a cocktail glass (*see left*)

**PRESENTATION**

Garnish with a sprig of mint

**DIFFICULTY**

Moderate

**STYLE**

A cocktail to drink on the porch

**TASTE**

Fresh and minty

**FINISH**

The gin dominates but the freshness remains

# Spitfire

## INGREDIENTS

40ml (1¼fl oz) Merlet Brothers Blend cognac, 30ml (1fl oz) lemon juice, 15ml (½fl oz) sugar syrup, 15ml (½fl oz) Merlet Crème de pêche, egg white, 30ml (1fl oz) dry white wine

With nothing new under the sun, everything's a variation on a theme. During the 1880s, a number of bartenders began to play with the traditional Whiskey Sour; once the cocktail was in the serving glass, they slowly added red wine to create a pretty halo to please the eyes as well as the tastebuds. This twist became known as the New York Sour and was considered by some to be the height of good taste. It is not that bad although a bit rough around the edges.

Well over a century later, Tony Conigliaro, one of the most interesting bartenders in London, transformed the Sour and delivered an ethereal cocktail, truly refined and delicious. He explains that each recipe has a formula which functions like a musical score: it can be interpreted in many ways, in many tones and registers. The distance between his Spitfire and the original is enormous, but the characteristics remain. Its base is a Sour made with cognac to which he adds a little Crème de pêche de vigne (vine peach liqueur). Instead of red wine, he adds white wine (Sicilian, although any decent dry white wine will do). The result is magic, both in terms of the texture and the flavour.

I discovered this cocktail in Tony's bar, 69 Colebrooke Row. It was not on the menu but when I asked the bartender to suggest something that would define the establishment, this is what he prepared for me. Conigliaro is, however, better known for his 'molecular' cocktails, even if he doesn't like the term. In any case I'm not complaining about the choice, and I feel sure you will understand. The Spitfire is a marvel, although it should not be confused with a cocktail of the same name, created by Harry MacElhone in London, 1941. That first Spitfire, a Sour with Scotch and sherry, is not at all bad but operates in quite a different style.

### PREPARATION

**Shake in a cocktail shaker (except for the wine)**

### TYPE OF GLASS

**Serve in a cocktail glass, carefully add the wine**

### DIFFICULTY

**Difficult**

### STYLE

**Fresh and ethereal cocktail**

### TASTE

**Wine and fruit (apricot), creamy**

**FINISH**

The peach gathers strength, then is balanced by the lemon and sugar

# 92 Straits Sling

INGREDIENTS

30ml (1fl oz) gin,
30ml (1fl oz) Cherry
Heering, 30ml (1fl oz)
Bénédictine, 30ml
(1fl oz) lime juice,
2 dashes Angostura
bitters, 2 dashes orange
bitters, soda water, lime
slice to serve

The Singapore Sling is the pride of the Raffles Hotel in Singapore, where it was invented by Ngiam Tong Boon sometime before 1915. But nobody can agree on his recipe. The International Bartenders Association suggests an indigestible mixture of gin, cherry brandy, Cointreau, Bénédictine, grenadine, pineapple juice and lime juice. For my part, I prefer to go back to what is perhaps the oldest version of this classic. It appeared in Robert Vermeire's 1922 book as the Straits Sling. Vermeire explains that this was a well-known drink from Singapore. Historically, a Sling was an ancestor of the cocktail, made with sugar, water and a liquor of some kind. This recipe is more complicated, although it is the height of simplicity compared to what it has become.

By removing the pineapple, triple sec and grenadine, you get something that is less tropical but infinitely more elegant – after all, the clientele of the Raffles Hotel were not particularly noted for wearing sandals, with or without socks, and flowered shirts. In any case this recipe corresponds almost exactly to one published in a Singapore newspaper in 1913 under the misleading name of Gin Sling, although Vermeire talks about lemon rather than lime. Here, however, I prefer to follow the journalist and tradition, especially since lime was not easily found in Europe during the 1920s.

When did the Straits Sling become the Singapore Sling? No idea. But I suspect the Mr Boon story to be essentially an invention *a posteriori*. Whatever the case, if you find yourself in Singapore and want to try the standard Singapore Sling, be aware that, due to demand, Raffles will serve it to you from a machine. Like a bad ice cream at a carnival. However, they say that it's always possible to persuade the bartender to prepare one for you himself.

PREPARATION

**Make directly in a Collins glass, serve over ice**

PRESENTATION

**Garnish with a slice of lime**

DIFFICULTY

**Moderate**

STYLE

**Fresh and complex cocktail**

TASTE

**Acid and herbaceous, almost medicinal**

FINISH

**Sugar and dried fruits, then slight tartness**

# 93 Tangerine

INGREDIENTS

30ml (1fl oz) Citadelle
gin, 15ml (½fl oz) St
Germain elderflower
liqueur, 2 teaspoons
rosemary syrup, 50ml
(1¾fl oz) clementine
juice, 15ml (½fl oz)
lime juice, egg white,
rosemary leaves to serve

Every year the alcohol industry launches an incredible amount of new products. But how many of them make a real impact and stand the test of time? Of all those launched over the last ten years, one seems to have got off to a good start: St Germain, an elderflower liqueur. It's a textbook case, launched by Rob Cooper, whose father had already managed to persuade everyone to buy Chambord, a raspberry liqueur inspired by one 'created on the occasion of a visit by Louis XIV'. Cooper's marketing pitch for St Germain tells us that the elderflowers are gathered by hand in the Alps by aged Frenchmen in berets who then bring their harvest home on bicycles. Yeah, yeah. Where they put their baguette and Camembert remains a mystery, about which, however, the enraptured consumers have every reason not to care. But you are free to believe it, of course.

In any case, it works: for some industry experts St Germain has managed to resuscitate the liqueur sector. If this is true, it is due not only – to be fair – to its history, whether true or not, nor to its splendid bottle; the fact is that it is an excellent product that works in almost all cocktails. And bartenders around the world have pounced upon it ever since it was introduced in 2007. It has even been called the 'bartender's ketchup', without that being in any way pejorative – the expression comes from the United States where, it seems, a good ketchup improves many a dish. To test it, I offer you this recipe created by Ruth Mateu in Spain in 2009. She was then working at Le Cabrera, when it set the benchmark for Madrid bars as well as being my second home – but where, sadly, it's no longer worth going. At the time the Tangerine was always very popular among people discovering the wonderful world of the cocktail for the first time.

PREPARATION

**Shake in a cocktail shaker**

TYPE OF GLASS

**Serve in a cocktail glass**

PRESENTATION

**Garnish with leaves of rosemary**

DIFFICULTY

**Difficult**

STYLE

**Fresh, light cocktail**

TASTE

**Round and fruity, with a floral touch**

FINISH

**Short, slightly herbaceous, lots of citrus**

# Tom Collins

### INGREDIENTS

60ml (2 fl oz) Old Tom
gin, 20ml (¾ fl oz) lemon
juice, 15ml (½ fl oz) sugar
syrup, soda water, lemon
peel or lime slice to serve

As we know, humour does not travel well. And the passing of time probably doesn't help. What must Americans of today think of their ancestors of 1874, when it was considered absolutely hilarious to ask a stranger if he had seen Tom Collins. 'Tom Collins? I don't know Tom Collins' was the inevitable response. The inveterate prankster would insist 'Well, you should go find him, because he's said some particularly insulting things about you.' A talented trickster would add layer upon layer to this opening gambit until his victim, red with rage, rushed off in pursuit of this accursed Tom Collins. Whereupon the gathering would finally roar with laughter and take the dupe's place at the counter ....

You won't be surprised to learn therefore that a Tom Collins appeared in an 1876 book of recipes. So what is it? A refreshing long drink, the perfect alternative to the Gin & Tonic and almost as simple to make. (The more perceptive among you will have noticed that the ingredients are the same as for a Gin Fizz, but the glass is larger and ice is added.) The way this relates to everything I have just told you is that there was already another Collins, first name John, in circulation in the United States during the 1860s. This one did not insult strangers (the name came from an English bartender), and was above all made with genever (Dutch gin). According to historian David Wondrich, the new name was due as much to the aforementioned hilarious prank as to the change of liquor, because friend Tom was made with gin ... Old Tom gin.

The Collins family has expanded since them: with each name having its own base spirit. But, no kidding, it's Tom that really works best. Incidentally, do you know Tom Collins? Because he told me that you make lousy cocktails....

PREPARATION

**Mix in a cocktail shaker (except for the soda water)**

TYPE OF GLASS

**Serve in a Collins glass filled with ice cubes, top up with soda water**

PRESENTATION

**Garnish with a twist of lemon peel or a slice of lime**

DIFFICULTY

**Moderate**

STYLE

**Refreshing long drink**

TASTE

**Sparkling lemonade bolstered by the gin**

FINISH

**Short and very slightly acid; a palate-cleanser**

# 95 Tommy's Margarita

INGREDIENTS
........................................

60ml (2fl oz) tequila
reposado, 30ml (1fl oz)
lime juice, 15ml (½fl oz)
agave nectar, lime slice
and zest to serve

A few years back, the 'healthy option' was to use agave syrup – natural, and therefore good for you – instead of sugar. Unfortunately agave has a very high fructose content, even more than those high-fructose corn syrups that make some sodas more dangerous than their calorie content might indicate. The lesson here is to beware of what is supposedly good for your health. The cocktail industry has its silly fashions, too.

If Tommy's Margarita is good for you, it's not down to its effect on your figure but on your taste buds. The Margarita is Mexico's iconic cocktail, despite the fact that no one knows who created it, or where, since none of the many stories told about it can be proved. The one sure thing is that an identical recipe, the Picador, appeared in London in 1937. However, Julio Bermejo, who created our recipe nearly twenty years ago, decided to take the Margarita and make it even more Mexican by ensuring that the spirit of the agave really stands out.

To do this, he got rid of the Cointreau with its orange notes and replaced the sugar with agave syrup. As you know, tequila is distilled from the agave plant, so the combination is ideal to really bring out the spirit's full qualities. (Don't forget, never use tequila that is less than 100 per cent agave). Add freshly squeezed lime juice and you have a splendidly refreshing cocktail, unpretentious but delicious and subtle. It's a Margarita reduced to the essentials. It can be found in many bars around the world but its home is Tommy's in San Francisco, a Mexican restaurant opened by Julio's parents in 1965. If you want to try the classic Margarita, use the following proportions: 50ml (1¾fl oz) tequila, 30ml (1fl oz) Cointreau and 15ml (½fl oz) lime juice. Frost the rim of a cocktail glass with salt, shake and serve.

**PREPARATION**

Shake in a cocktail shaker

**TYPE OF GLASS**

Serve in an Old Fashioned glass filled with ice cubes

**PRESENTATION**

Garnish with lime zest and a slice of lime

**DIFFICULTY**

Moderate

**STYLE**

Mexican classic

**TASTE**

Intense vegetable notes, acidulous

FINISH

The wood appears, long on agave and citrus

# Vesper

## INGREDIENTS

60ml (2fl oz) G'Vine
Nouaison gin, 20ml
(¾fl oz) Ciroc vodka,
2 teaspoons Lillet,
lemon peel to serve

James Bond may be forever associated with a not terribly good Dry Martini (made with vodka and shaken), but his eye strayed to other drinks, too. We know he had a predilection for bourbon and Champagne and the first ever cocktail he consumed was an Americano, at the beginning of *Casino Royale*, the first of Ian Fleming's fourteen novels. It was also in this book that he committed the greatest infidelity to the Martini and to his principles; he created a cocktail for a woman with whom he would fall in love. The story is well known: after gambling at the casino in Royale-les-Eaux, Bond goes to the bar with Felix Leiter, his CIA counterpart. He orders a Dry Martini in a Champagne goblet before changing his mind and asking the bartender for a drink of his own invention: three measures of gin, one of vodka and a half-measure of Lillet, garnished with a large thin slice of lemon peel.

At this point the drink does not yet have a name. It is christened only later, when Bond decides to call it a Vesper, in honour of the first Bond Girl (played in the 2006 movie by Eva Green, no less). After *Casino Royale*, Bond never again drinks a Vesper. All the same, it is undoubtedly the second cocktail most closely associated with him. The irony is two-fold: Fleming, interviewed in 1958, mentions a cocktail created for Bond, which he personally found awful. The Vesper? Undoubtedly. Conclusion: Bond loves fast cars, pretty ladies and good wines but as far as cocktails are concerned he cannot be relied upon (after all, he's not American).

That said, Fleming exaggerated. The Vesper is not undrinkable. It's just that, for someone accustomed to the Martini, it's difficult to see the added value. On the other hand it's an excellent stop along the road to redemption for fans of vermouth-free Vodkatinis.

**PREPARATION**

**Shake in a cocktail shaker**

**TYPE OF GLASS**

**Serve in a cocktail or Martini glass**

**PRESENTATION**

**Garnish with a twist of lemon peel**

**DIFFICULTY**

**Moderate**

**STYLE**

**Strong dry aperitif**

**TASTE**

**Light, with a strong gin presence and orange notes**

**FINISH**

**Discreet and clean, fairly dry**

# Vieux Carré

### INGREDIENTS

30ml (1fl oz) Merlet
Brothers Blend cognac,
30ml (1fl oz) rye whiskey,
30ml (1fl oz) red
vermouth, 2 teaspoons
Bénédictine, 1 dash
Angostura bitters,
2 dashes Peychaud's
bitters, lemon peel or
1 maraschino cherry
to serve

If you don't remember or have yet to read the details of the La Louisiane cocktail, (re)read it now: the Vieux Carré is its logical sequel. New Orleans is a city famous for partying and excess. It's easy to imagine to what degree Prohibition must have seemed like a spanner in the works. No problem: the city soon became contrabrand central. One of the 'super agents' tracking the bootleggers would time how long it took to find alcohol (and thus make an arrest) in the towns he visited. New Orleans held the absolute record, with thirty-five … seconds!

A well-known bar called the Old Absinthe House was closed in 1926 because it broke the law. Perhaps it was due to this insistence on continuing as before that the classic formulas of the American cocktail were not forgotten during the twelve-year enforced drought. This Vieux Carré is the proof: documented for the first time in 1937, it was created sometime after 1933 by Walter Bergeron (not to be confused with his namesake Victor, better known as Trader Vic), who was at the time bartender at the Monteleone Hotel. His cocktail respects all the rules of the classic Creole cocktail. In fact, although made with different proportions and served differently, it includes all the ingredients of La Louisiane, with the addition of cognac, which was, as we have seen, the preferred spirit of the New Orleansians during the first half of the 19th century.

Try both cocktails, one after the other. You will notice not only the resemblance but also the differences, albeit very slight at first sight. The Monteleone is still open today but since 1949 its bar has been named the Carousel. With reason: it's a real merry-go-round, a 25-seat revolving carousel bar. It is also the nerve centre for Tales of the Cocktail®, the world's premier cocktail festival, held every July.

**PREPARATION**

**Stir in a mixing glass**

**TYPE OF GLASS**

**Serve in an Old Fashioned glass filled with ice cubes**

**PRESENTATION**

**Garnish with a maraschino cherry or a twist of lemon peel**

**DIFFICULTY**

**Moderate**

**STYLE**

**Full-bodied cocktail**

**TASTE**

**Ample. Herbaceous and spicy but also sugary**

**FINISH**

**Long. The bitterness and spices (clove) combine with cognac notes**

# 98 Waterloo

### INGREDIENTS

45ml (1½fl oz) gin, 20ml (¾fl oz) sugar syrup, 15ml (½fl oz) lemon juice, 15ml (½fl oz) Campari, 4 chunks of watermelon plus extra to serve

Many of the preceding cocktails have used herbs, spices and even muddled citrus fruits. However, other fruits can also add an extra dimension to your drinks, without falling into the trap of adding sugary fruit juice to hide the taste of alcohol in cocktails embellished with kitsch paper umbrellas. Watermelon, for example, deserves to be popularized beyond poor Daiquiris or Mojitos.

The Waterloo is a fine example of the possibilities of this fruit when selected ripe, in full season. It is one of the bestsellers on the summer menu at Employees Only, a New York bar that serves more than 130,000 cocktails a year. Over there, they know their stuff, and not only in terms of cocktails: realizing that their patrons also come to meet people, the layout is designed so that everyone seated at the bar can see all his/her neighbours. There are no blind spots.

Constructed with a classic base of gin, sugar syrup and lemon juice, the Waterloo is lengthened with the juice of 4 chunks of watermelon that have been muddled in the bottom of the shaker (and further by shaking). To give the mixture a little more depth, the stroke of genius (and this is the mark of a true pro) was to add 15ml (½fl oz) of Campari, which accentuates the colour and brings a sharp contrast that makes the cocktail even more refreshing (the popularity of ultra-sweet drinks in high summer remains a mystery...). The combination of watermelon and Campari works genuine miracles. The bartenders at Employees Only advise not straining the cocktail and leaving the watermelon seeds in the serving glass. The visual effect is not bad but since the cocktail is drunk through a straw you may find it a bit annoying. It's up to you.

**PREPARATION**

Shake in a cocktail shaker (see left)

**TYPE OF GLASS**

Serve in a Collins glass

**PRESENTATION**

Garnish with a wedge of watermelon

**DIFFICULTY**

Difficult

**STYLE**

Long summer drink

**TASTE**

Luscious, with a slight bitterness

**FINISH**

Medium long and refreshing, watermelon and citrus

# 99 Whisk(e)y Sour

60ml (2fl oz) whisk(e)y,
30ml (1fl oz) lemon
juice, 15ml (½fl oz)
sugar syrup, 1 egg white
(optional), 1 maraschino
cherry to serve and
lemon slice to serve

What's in a letter? Whiskey for American and Irish whiskey and whisky for Scotch whisky (and the rest of the world). Of course, the Sour can be made with any kind of spirits – versions are found made with gin, rum, calvados, cognac, tequila – and no matter what syrup (grenadine, orgeat) or even with a liqueur.

Accordingly, for the Whisky/Whiskey Sour, choose the brand that appeals to you at the time. I would suggest an elegant yet robust whisk(e)y. Beyond this, the formula I propose here is the recipe in its most basic but also its most essential form: the perfect balance between the lemon and the sugar, the ideal platform for the greatest miracles of mixology.

The proportions are mine; yours may be different. Nevertheless, bear one thing in mind: if the acidity is not to destroy what is left of your dental enamel, don't put in too much sugar. This cocktail first appeared in 1856 and was one of the most popular for nearly a century. Even now it is one of those whose name is familiar to non-initiates, although obviously it comes way behind Martinis, Mojitos, Daiquiris or Piña Coladas in the fame stakes. In the US, motherland of the Whiskey Sour with an 'e', it is served either in a stemmed glass (without ice) or in a whisky glass (without 'e' but with ice cubes). Depending on whether you want to drink it quickly or sip it tranquilly, both options are good. The Whisk(e)y Sour holds no secret, especially if you have already read the (nearly) 100 recipes that precede it.

All the same, allow me to slip you a bit of advice, a recommendation made, I am proud to reveal, by Robert Vermeire, another Belgian, in 1922: add an egg white to make your Sour … silky.

### PREPARATION
**Shake in a cocktail shaker**

### TYPE OF GLASS
**Serve in an Old Fashioned or a cocktail glass (see left)**

### PRESENTATION
**Garnish with a maraschino cherry and slice of lemon**

### DIFFICULTY
**Moderate**

### STYLE
**Robust but easy cocktail**

### TASTE
**Acidic but balanced, vanilla notes from the bourbon**

**FINISH**

**Freshness of the lemon, length of the wood**

# 100 White Russian

## INGREDIENTS

50ml (1¾fl oz) vodka,
20ml (¾fl oz) coffee
liqueur, 30ml (1fl oz)
cream or crème fraîche

You may think of James Bond with a Vesper, or Grace Kelly with a Martini, or even Alec Guinness enjoying a Daiquiri, but for my generation the cocktail + movie reference is very different: a slightly paunchy old hippie in sandals making a mixture of vodka, coffee liqueur and – laziness being at its peak and the refrigerator decidedly empty – powdered milk. Help! Even the fact that someone has just stolen a rug that 'tied the room together' is no excuse.

But for fans of *The Big Lebowski*, the Dude can get away with anything and a significant number of its fans not only returned to bowling but even demanded White Russians from bar staff only familiar with Heineken or Stella. With such a title, you might think the drink references some novel about Russian émigré circles in Berlin just after the Bolshevik revolution. In fact the name has much more prosaic origins. Let's see now, a Russian spirit, the colour white – the post-WWII cocktail crisis was in all respects a crisis of imagination.

If you omit the cream you will have … keep guessing … a Black Russian, invented in 1949 by Gustave Tops, the inspired bartender of Brussels' Métropole Hotel. Apparently, its white cousin did not appear until fifteen years later, but rather like the Dude, I simply don't have the energy to go and check. If you too feel a trifle fragile and want a White Russian, at least save your last reserves of strength to pour the fresh cream over the mixture of coffee liqueur and vodka with care. Otherwise, as well as not being particularly good, your Russian will not be very white: it will just be deeply unattractive.

PREPARATION

**Mix in an Old Fashioned glass (except the cream), serve over ice cubes and carefully add the cream**

DIFFICULTY

**Moderate**

STYLE

**Digestif cocktail**

TASTE

**Café crème with ethanol**

FINISH

**Brief, on the milk and yet again the coffee**

# 101 Zombie

45ml (1½fl oz) Puerto
Rican rum, 45ml
(1½fl oz) Jamaican rum,
30ml (1fl oz) Demerara
Overproof rum, 30ml
(1fl oz) lime juice, 15ml
(½fl oz) Falernum,
2 teaspoons yellow
grapefruit juice,
1 teaspoon cinnamon
syrup, 1 teaspoon
grenadine, 6 drops
absinthe, 1 dash
Angostura bitters, mint
sprig or pineapple slice
to serve

There is a bit of a contradiction in ending a book that aims to introduce accessible and relatively simple cocktails with the Zombie. Just look at the list of ingredients! In my defence I offer several arguments, the easiest first: the Zombie, now there's a well-thought-out name with which to end a book of cocktail recipes. One hundred and one cocktails! They would have a dangerous effect on even the most practised of drinkers. More seriously, if you are still with me and have tried most of the cocktails on offer so far, you will have acquired some experience and not a little skill. It may be time to move up a level and to take an interest in rarer ingredients, such as overproof rums (over 70 per cent alcohol) or falernum (a syrup, sometimes slightly alcoholic, made with lime and sugar and flavoured with almond and spices such as ginger or cloves) and to think of making your own syrups, such as cinnamon.

Next, if I am able to offer you the authentic Zombie recipe, hitherto kept secret for a very long time, it is thanks to the tireless efforts of Jeff Berry (ten years of research!). Every entry in this book owes something to one or other of mixology's enthusiasts and history nuts, such as David Wondrich, Philip Greene and Fernando Castellon. When you sip your Zombie think about them as much as about the bartenders, anonymous or otherwise, who have created these recipes. But especially remember the advice of Don the Beachcomber: don't drink more than two, because that would turn you into a real zombie.

That recommendation in itself justifies the inclusion of this cocktail at the end of the book: it is up to us to drink responsibly, so that it always remains a pleasure.

**PREPARATION**

**Mix in a blender**

**TYPE OF GLASS**

**Serve in a Hurricane or Collins glass. Add ice if necessary**

**PRESENTATION**

**Garnish with a sprig of mint or a slice of pineapple**

**DIFFICULTY**

**Difficult**

**STYLE**

**Last cocktail for the road**

**TASTE**

**Surprising: easy despite the alcohol; spicy**

**FINISH**

Slightly piquant, almond, cinnamon and clove dominate

# Cocktail
# Techniques

# Cocktail Techniques

Reading *101 Cocktails to Try Before You Die* will not turn you into a professional shaker. That is not the aim of this book, and the techniques needed to make the various cocktails included here are not numerous. The important thing is to be able to reproduce them at home without too much difficulty. These basic principles regarding equipment, ice, glasses and methods should prove helpful.

## EQUIPMENT
To make the 101 cocktails, in addition to the usual cooking equipment that most people have, you will need:

- **A shaker.** There are many kinds on the market. Beginners will prefer a three-piece shaker with built-in strainer.

- **A mixing glass.** This is used to prepare cocktails that are stirred, not shaken. Boston cocktail shakers consist of a metal bottom and a glass top, which could be used as a mixing glass. However, the Boston is a rather complicated shaker for beginners.

- **A measure.** Also called a jigger. Cheap measures often have one cup that measures 2cl/25ml/¾fl oz and one that measures 4cl/50ml/1¾fl oz (more common for UK/US). They may not be all that accurate but they are indispensable – measuring by sight is not a good idea. If you are prepared to spend a little more it is worthwhile. Some jiggers have grooves that indicate fractions of measures. You could also use kitchen measures but they will slow down your mixing.

- **A bar spoon.** Longer than a normal spoon, it enables you to stir your creations in the mixing glass. The bowl's capacity is generally that of a teaspoon.

- **A strainer.** This is a sieve designed for serving cocktails while holding back the ice cubes in Boston-style shakers or mixing glasses.

- **A conical strainer.** This should be used when the cocktails contain fresh herbs or fruit so that you don't end up with pieces of either in the glass.

- **A muddler.**

- **A blender** (for three cocktails).

## ICE CUBES

You probably don't realise it but, apart from the quality of the ingredients, ice cubes are the main culprit in a bad cocktail. The quickest way to an unpleasant taste experience is to use ice cubes made in traditional moulds that have been cosying up to your frozen cod. And even if your ice cubes are good, if you use too few, your cocktail will not be cold enough or adequately diluted (dilution is necessary, but needs to be controlled). If you buy your ice cubes in a shop, opt for the solid ones (i.e. not hollow). To store them, avoid the meat or fish compartment of your refrigerator and use them as quickly as possible. You can buy large ice-cube trays online for making ice cubes at home. To ensure you have enough, store some you have made earlier in a clean Tupperware container. When making cocktails, always fill the shaker or mixing glass at least three-quarters full of ice. Don't try to cut back on this, you will taste the difference.

## METHODS
### In the shaker

Once the ice and ingredients are inside, make sure the lid is on securely. Shake it with an energetic but regular forward-backward movement of the wrists for 10–15 seconds. When the sides of a metal shaker start to feel intensely cold, it's time to serve the cocktail. There's no need to shake frenziedly, but the ice cubes and the liquid should circulate well inside the shaker (you should hear the sound of ice cubes regularly hitting the sides of the shaker as you move it back and forth).

### In the mixing glass

The principle is simple: add the ingredients, then fill up with ice cubes; use the mixing spoon to stir with a circular movement, from the bottom of the glass to the top, for twenty seconds. In terms of chilling, the mixing glass is less effective than the shaker. It is generally used for cocktails that do not contain juice, to obtain a clear and elegant cocktail (a Martini made in a shaker, for example, would be cloudy with a slight foam on the surface).

### Directly in the serving glass

Here the cocktail is 'built' by adding each ingredient to the serving glass already filled with ice cubes. Stir briefly and add more ice if necessary.

### In the blender

In addition to the ingredients, add enough crushed ice to equal the capacity of the serving glass. Run the blender for 5–10 seconds at top speed. Note that the Cubans add the spirits gradually, as if they were the oil in a mayonnaise.

## GLASSWARE

Many different glasses can be used to serve cocktails. In this book I suggest essentially the three following kinds:

- Cocktail/goblet/hurricane/Martini glass: this means a stemmed glass with a capacity of 100–150ml (3½–5fl oz). The characteristic Martini glass is V-shaped. High-alcohol cocktails, without juice, should be served in glasses of maximum 100–120ml (3½–4fl oz) capacity.

- Collins glass: for long drinks/highball, with a capacity of around 300ml (10fl oz/½ pint).

- Old Fashioned or Rocks glass: a whisky glass with a capacity of 200–300ml (7–10fl oz).

... but you can be creative.

## ESSENTIAL ADVICE

- Lemon, lime, orange and grapefruit juice should always be freshly squeezed. It's OK to buy pineapple juice, but without added sugar.

- Unless expressly specified, always strain your cocktail in order to leave the ice cubes in the mixing glass or shaker. The cocktails in this book are most often served 'up', i.e. on fresh ice cubes.

- Cocktails containing egg white or a whole egg should first be shaken without ice cubes in order to obtain an emulsion. Then add ice cubes and proceed as normal. Alternatively, you could use a milk frother, which will make the dry shake unnecessary.

- When soda water is specified for a cocktail prepared in a shaker, it should not be shaken with the other ingredients but added directly to the serving glass once the contents of the shaker have been poured into it.

- Any citrus peel used as garnish should be cut with the least amount of pith possible, then expressed over the cocktail so that the essential oils will float on the surface.

- When using a leaf or sprig of an aromatic herb to garnish your cocktail, first put it on your palm and give it a light slap to release its aroma.

- The way to use a pestle depends on the ingredient to be crushed. Herbs (basil, mint, etc.) should be handled with care to avoid any bitterness. With pieces of fruit, on the other hand, it's necessary to extract all the juice.

- When making a cocktail straight into the serving glass, first put in the ice cubes before adding the ingredients, except when it's necessary to crush herbs or fruit.

- When making a cocktail directly in a glass with crushed ice, if the ice does not come up to the rim of the glass after stirring, add more before inserting straws and/or the garnish.

# Glossary

**Bitters**
Bitter aromatic concentrates that serve to unite different elements of a recipe and to give a bit more complexity and depth to cocktails. They come in many flavours.

**Maraschino cherry**
A stoned cherry that has been steeped in maraschino liqueur, brandy or other spirits. Avoid artificially coloured confectioner's cherries.

**Falernum**
A sweet, sometimes slightly alcoholic syrup, made with lemon, almonds and spices (ginger, clove, Jamaican pepper ...).

**Frosting**
A technique that consists of running a lemon or lime wedge around the rim of the glass, then dipping the rim in salt or sugar. Typical of the Margarita or Sidecar.

**Kina**
Or chinchona. A wine-based aperitif, such as Lillet or Dubonnet, chiefly flavoured with chinchona bark.

**Maraschino**
A liqueur originating in Dalmatia, made from a distillation of marasca cherries. Clear and herbaceous, it is essential for classic cocktails.

**Mezcal**
A cousin of tequila, distilled from the maguey plant, a type of agave. Smokier and stronger than tequila, it can be used in all 'tequila classics' and in an ever-increasing number of cocktail creations.

**Orgeat**
A sweet syrup made from almonds and sugar, generally prepared with a little orange flower water.

### Sherry
Fortified Spanish wines. They range from very dry (Fino) to very sweet (Pedro Ximenez).

### Sugar syrup
Commercially available but very easy to make at home. Dilute 2 parts of sugar in 1 part of water (in volume) and heat very gently. It will keep for a month in the refrigerator, in a sterilized bottle.

### Speakeasy
An illicit bar in the Prohibition era in the United States. Also used for contemporary 'fake' clandestine bars that play on the image of that dark time.

### Swizzle
A small stick with three or five branches, often used to stir certain tropical cocktails.

### Tiki
A style of tropical cocktail, often rum-based, created in the United States after Prohibition and inspired by South Pacific culture.

### Up (or Straight Up)
Meaning that the cocktail is served without ice in the glass.

### Vermouth
Wine-based aperitif, chiefly flavoured with Artemesia.

# Index by alcohol

# Photo credits

**123RF** Fedor Kondratenko 30; Thorben Maier 74, 78. **Alamy** Duncan Johnson/ Cephas Picture Library 210. **Aviation Gin** 10, 20, 26, 32, 62, 114, 124, 146. **Cocteleria Creativa by George Restrepo** 36, 106. **Dreamstime.com** Ivan Mateev 16; Martiapunts 178; Maxim Tatarinov 132; Mohd Oqba Bin Abdul Malek 204; Wollertz 122. **Eurowinegate** 70, 144. **Ferrand** 48, 90, 186, 188. **Fotolia** Atiketta Sangsaeng 80; Blazer76 28, 132; Boris Ryzhkov 158; Dimitry Lobanov 52; Igor Klimov 152; innervisionpro 96; Kondor83 2, 9; Lidi 154; Palle Christensen 68, 162; Scomorokh 94, 120; wollertz 12, 50, 76, 182. **Getty Images** Rita Maas 156; Sheri L Giblin 180. **Graphic Obsession** FoodCollection 196. **Havana Club** 130, 136. **iStockphoto.com** gpalmer1477 88, 208; hayesphotography 86; iaartist 38, 40; iodrakon 138; Ivanmateev 116; jcphoto 128; mitchellpictures 208; pjohnson1 198; rgbdigital 19. **Jamie Boudreau** 172. **Julien Escot** 54. **Laurence Marot** 24. **Luke Kirwan** 56. **Matthias Friedlein** 148. **Mayte Esbri** 104, 112, 170, 184. **Monti** 13, 25, 82, 84, 104. **Merlet** 44, 150. 190, 202. **Nick Brown** 142. **Octopus Publishing Group** Cristian Barnett 166; Jonathan Kennedy 102; Sandra Lane 176; Stephen Conroy 8, 14, 72; William Reavell 206. **Ruben de Gracia** 100. **Ruth Mateu** 194. **Shutterstock** Foodio 64; Mateusz Gzik 29. **Simona Belotti** 174.

Any images not included above belong to their respective authors. We did our utmost to obtain the necessary permissions to secure reproduction rights for images for this book. Any omission should be brought to our attention and will be rectified in the next edition.